The New Protective State

Government, intelligence and terrorism

Edited by

PETER HENNESSY

D1342378

continuum

Continuum
The Tower Building, 11 York Road, London SE1 7NX
80 Maiden Lane, Suite 704, New York NY 10038

Published by Continuum Books in association with the
Mile End Institute

www.continuumbooks.com

First published 2007

British Library Cataloguing-in-Publication Data
A catalogue record for this book is available from the British Library.

ISBN: 0–8264–9614–8

Typeset by Kenneth Burnley, Wirral, Cheshire
Printed and bound in Great Britain by MPG Books Ltd,
Bodmin, Cornwall

2/23

Contents

Contents

Introduction

The intelligence profession, like most other forms of organized human activity, is very often shaped by powerful weather-makers. For the bulk of the years since 1945 it was the potential military threat posed by the Soviet Union, its allies and the ideology which appeared to drive the Eastern Bloc's approaches to international affairs. For a brief and, from today's perspective, rather strange decade after the hardliners' coup failed in Moscow in August 1991, there was no single dominant weather-maker to condition life and thought within the British and Western intelligence communities. Since September 2001, there has been.

As in the early years of the Cold War, people and systems have taken a while to absorb the nature, magnitude and likely duration of the new threat from international terrorism on a scale not previously experienced by any of the countries which are its potential targets. As Dame Eliza Manningham-Buller points out in her chapter, in the autumn of 2006 all the British agencies, departments and authorities involved in countering international terrorism were still climbing a steep learning-curve. This book, largely created by serving or former intelligence practitioners or customers of the intelligence product, traces the analytical and, in part, philosophical developments in British thinking five years on from the attacks on the Twin Towers in New York and the Pentagon in Washington.

It chiefly consists of papers or lectures presented to the Mile End Group which is run by and for research students in the Department of History at Queen Mary, University of London, during the course of 2006. The MEG is part of the Mile End Institute for the Study of Government, Intelligence and Society. This study, in partnership with Continuum, is the Institute's first publication. Some of the contributions had, in an earlier form, been presented to other bodies. For example, Chapter 5 was originally presented by Sir David Omand at Gresham College to the Gresham Society as the Peter Nailor Memorial Lecture in 2005. And Chapter 6 was first read by Sir Michael Quinlan as the 2005 Annual Lecture to the Centre for Intelligence Studies in the Department of International Relations at the University of Wales, Aberystwyth.

The book is intended to be a contribution both to contemporary history and what Fernand Braudel liked to call 'slower pulse'[1] varieties of the discipline. For just as today's research students, pursuing the still-young trade of British intelligence history, now cut their intellectual teeth on the once tightly protected archives whose files reflect the adjustment to a long and sometimes dangerous Cold War in the late 1940s, scholars of the mid-twentieth century may well be fascinated to see how the new UK protective state was created in the early years of the new millennium. This book, its authors hope, will endure as an aid to their attempts to reconstruct the analyses, approaches and systems of those who strove to build it.

As this book went to press in the first days of March 2007, there was much speculation in the press and in Whitehall about possible reconfigurations of the machinery of government for dealing with counter-terrorism. But the Cabinet had yet to discuss a final resolution of the possibilities.[2] The chief purpose

1   Fernand Braudel, *A History of Civilizations* (London: Penguin, 1995), p. xxxvii.
2   Peter Riddell, 'Home Office is at the heart of a turf war over anti-terrorism', *The Times*, 1 March 2007.

of this book, whatever the future might hold, is to portray the thinking of a range of key insiders (the editor apart) in 2006 about the first five years on the road from 9/11.

Mile End Institute, Queen Mary, University of London
March 2007

1

From Secret State to Protective State

Peter Hennessy

. . . the destabilizing and hence conflict-engendering consequences of developing technology . . . [means] . . . aggression will continue to trump defence, but the means of aggression will become increasingly cheap, widely available and so to speak portable; this diffusion will almost inevitably in the end lead to these means coming into the possession of someone inclined, through fanaticism or folly, to deploy them.

(Ernest Gellner, 1991)[1]

In 1991, the great social anthropologist Ernest Gellner published an essay entitled 'War and Violence'. Characteristically, it was as perceptive about the recently ended Cold War as it was prescient about the anxieties and threats generated by international terrorism and potentially rogue states a decade later. Gellner was especially well placed to write on such themes, for he was as well primed on the Soviet Union and

1   Ernest Gellner, *Anthropology and Politics: Revolutions in the Sacred Grove* (Oxford: Blackwell, 1995), p. 171. His essay was originally published as 'An Anthropological View of War and Violence' in Robert A. Hinde (ed.), *The Institution of War* (London: Comminan, 1991), pp. 62–80.

Eastern Europe as on the politics and anthropology of the Middle East and Muslim societies generally.[2]

This is what he wrote about Cold War past and its nuclear dimension:

> The powerful and destructive weapons were so complex that they could only be acquired in any large quantity by a very small number of superpowers. These tend to be endowed with at least relatively pacific populations: the new weapons could only be produced by industrial machines, whose members are not literally warriors in any old sense, but instead are highly trained technical personnel, whose work and education incline them to lead inherently pacific lives.[3]

Gellner was no Pollyanna, but he did not see the political leaderships of the original nuclear-tipped powers as 'madmen in all authority . . . distilling their frenzy' (in Keynes' marvellous phrase)[4] into a succession of high-risk actions. 'The authorities in the superpowers in question', Gellner judged,

> were also at least relatively rational and moderate: they were not, by temperament or ethos, committed either to a cult of wild risk-taking as inherently admirable and noble, nor were they, whatever their formal pronounce-

---

2   Gellner's books included *Muslim Society* (Cambridge: CUP, 1981); *Nations and Nationalism* (Blackwell, 1983); *Culture, Identity and Politics* (CUP, 1987); *Plough, Sword and Book* (London: CollinsHarvill, 1988); *Relativism and the Social Sciences* (CUP, 1985); *Language and Solitude* (CUP, 1998); *Conditions of Liberty: Civil Society and Its Rivals* (London: Hamish Hamilton, 1994).

3   Gellner, *Anthropology and Politics*, p. 170.

4   J. M. Keynes, *The General Theory of Employment, Interest and Money* (London: Macmillan, 1936), p. 383.

ments, fanatical enough to fight for their belief system irrespective of risk.[5]

In the early 1990s, Gellner was well aware that '[a]ll these assumptions may in due course cease to hold'; that hugely destructive weapons might no longer be so difficult to manufacture to the point where 'they may become increasingly available by purchase, or even by local production, even to societies whose members are not pervaded by a relatively pacific, productive ethos'. Gellner recognized, too,

> that, while a large armoury may be needed if there is to be any prospect of victory and survival, a much smaller one will do for a determined blackmailer. He knows that his success will depend on the credibility of his threat. He will realize that his threat will only carry conviction if *he really does mean it*, whatever the cost to *him* if his bluff is called. He may be willing to pay that price, even though he knows that, if his bluff is indeed called, he will himself perish together with his enemies.[6]

Gellner concluded that as 'the proliferation of high-tech weapons proceeds, the probability of some of them being acquired by groups endowed with such a state of mind eventually becomes very great. The present [i.e. early-1990s] increase in international terrorism offers a small but frightening foretaste, as yet on only a moderate scale, of such a situation.'[7]

Ernest Gellner died in November 1995. He did not live to see the jihadist terrorist attacks on New York and Washington in September 2001 or those in London in July 2005. Nor did

---

5 Gellner, *Anthropology and Politics*, p. 170.
6 *Ibid.*, pp. 170–1.
7 *Ibid.*, p. 171.

he develop his contrast between Cold War politico-social anthropology and that of the different age of anxiety through which we are now living, though it could to some extent be foreseen, as Gellner himself sensed, in the last years of his life.

That contrast – both in terms of similarities and differences – is the theme of this chapter. The idea of such an exercise was stimulated by an event, a process and an observation. The event took place in Whitehall during the first days after the atrocity of 11 September 2001 when the Secretary of the Cabinet, Sir Richard Wilson, sent for the old Cold War files on what to do if the Prime Minister was wiped out by a bolt-from-the-blue attack. In the autumn of 1961, following a review stimulated by Lord Mountbatten, Chief of the Defence Staff, a policy was adopted of nominating two 'alternative' decision-takers from among the senior ministerial ranks for the purposes of authorizing nuclear retaliation. When the relevant file was declassified in August 2006, it showed a macabre, Shakespearean side to Macmillan. Asked by the Cabinet Office to nominate his two nuclear deputies, he scribbled this on the bottom of the minute:

> I agree the following –
>
> First Gravedigger   Mr Butler
> Second Gravedigger   Mr Lloyd
>
> HM
> 6/10/61

('Quite obviously,' John Ramsden said on reading this extraordinary document, 'Macmillan was casting himself as Hamlet. What other Prime Minister would have done that?')[8]

---

8 National Archives, Public Record Office, CAB 21, London and Oxford: 6081, Bishop to Macmillan, 5 October 1961; Macmillan to Bishop, 6 October 1961. For the original 'gravediggers' see *The Works of William*

This 'gravediggers' one-and-two practice had lapsed in the decade between the failure of the hardliners' coup in Moscow in August 1991 and the attack on the Twin Towers and the Pentagon. On the advice of Sir Richard Wilson, it was restored by the Prime Minister, Tony Blair, in 2001. Now, as in the 1960s, 1970s and 1980s, the choice of alternatives is made on an *ad hominem* basis rather than ministerial job or place in the Government's order or precedence.[9]

The process part of the stimulus for this chapter (of which details of the 1960–1 review of nuclear retaliation procedures formed a part), was the surge of Cold War-related documentary releases under the 'Waldegrave Initiative'.[10] This started during the second Major Government and grew apace in the late 1990s and early 2000s. It enabled scholars for the first time to piece together the hidden structures and the concealed details of Britain's Cold War secrets, as some of the most sensitive files retained beyond the normal 30 years reached the Public Record Office at Kew.[11] My research students and I, therefore, were embarked on a process of scholarly catch-up on these highly revealing papers just as early-twenty-first-century Whitehall was beginning to build the new protective state in response to the threat posed by al-Qaeda, its adherents and its imitators.

The observation, which joined the event and the process as the trigger for this volume, was a remark of Richard Wilson's, when Cabinet Secretary, during a briefing he gave to my students (which, in retirement, he has made public).[12] The

---

Shakespeare (Shakespeare Head Press/Blackwell, 1938), 'Hamlet', Act V, Scene 1, lines 1–231. See also Peter Hennessy, *The Secret State: Whitehall and the Cold War* (London: Penguin, 2003), pp. 154–65; conversation with Professor John Ramsden, 17 August 2006.

9 Private information.

10 Peter Hennessy, *The Prime Minister: The Office and Its Holders Since 1945* (London: Penguin, 2001).

11 Hennessy, *The Secret State*.

12 Lord Wilson of Dinton, 'Tomorrow's Government', Royal Society of Arts Lecture, 1 March 2006.

British, Lord Wilson said, have the habit of going into their big changes 'as if under anaesthetic'. (He had in mind the UK's accession to the European Economic Community in the early 1970s and the devolution legislation plus Human Rights Act in the late 1990s.) Only much later, he explained, do people realize the significance of these huge constitutional changes and tend to ask 'Is that what we really meant?'

To my mind, the construction of the wider protective state since 2001 falls into this 'anaesthetic' category. Parliament, public and the press have yet to appreciate fully either its scope and magnitude in-the-round or its long-term significance to our systems of government and the kind of country we are. My purpose in this chapter, therefore, is to compare and contrast the UK's Cold War secret state of 1948–91 with the new protective state of 2001 and after, then turning to the wider and enduring importance of what has been built and what is still under construction.

Threats and responses

The State is the coldest of cold monsters.

(General Charles de Gaulle)[13]

The state's apparatus comes no colder than those of its moving parts where intelligence, threat assessments, counter-measures and contingency planning meet and intersect. This was as true during the great 40-year East–West confrontation as it has been post-2001 when the UK and its allies have had to contend with terrorism of a magnitude and kind which distinguishes it from anything heretofore experienced even by those countries, like Britain, with a long history of coping with it.

---

13   Attributed to Charles de Gaulle.

The state that was pieced together very rapidly after the Berlin blockade was begun by the Soviets in June 1948 and that developed over the decades that followed until the Berlin Wall came down in November 1989 could, without exaggeration, have been described as cold, monstrous *and* secretive. The post-2001 protective state may deserve the first two adjectives but the third, in relative terms, does not apply. The degree of openness about the bulk of it (the sources and methods of intelligence-gathering and certain protective measures and plans understandably excepted) has been both noticeable and, by previous UK standards, remarkable.

At no stage during the Cold War, for example, was a White Paper published which came near to matching *Countering International Terrorism: The United Kingdom's Strategy* of July 2006.[14] Its only Cold War rival in terms of candour about the vulnerability of the UK was the famous Sandys Defence White Paper of 1957.[15]

Compare the 1957 paragraph which historians, rightly, have agreed contributed powerfully to the creation of the Campaign for Nuclear Disarmament the following year,[16] with the threat assessment contained in the 2006 counter-terrorism White Paper.

First the 1987 document:

It must be frankly recognized that there is at present no means of providing adequate protection for the people of this country against the consequences of an attack with nuclear weapons. Though in the event of war, the fighter aircraft of

---

14 *Countering International Terrorism: The United Kingdom's Strategy*, Cm 6888 (London: Stationery Office, July 2006).
15 *Defence: Outline of Future Policy*, Cmnd 124 (London: HMSO, 1957).
16 Christopher Driver, *The Disarmers: A Study in Protest* (London: Hodder, 1964), pp. 42–53; see also the MI5 brief on the history of CND prepared for Harold Macmillan in 1963 in NA, PRO, PREM 11/4285, 'The Development of the Nuclear Disarmament Movement', April 1963.

the RAF would unquestionably take a heavy toll of enemy
bombers, a proportion would inevitably get through. Even if
it were only a dozen, they could with megaton [i.e. hydrogen]
bombs inflict widespread devastation.[17]

Now the 2006 assessment:

The Government assesses that the current threat in the
UK from Islamist terrorism is serious and sustained.
British citizens also face the threat of terrorist attacks
when abroad. Overall, we judge that the scale of the
threat is potentially still increasing and is not likely to
diminish significantly for some years.

The UK has achieved some significant successes in
dealing with potential attacks by Islamist terrorists, since
before 2001. A number of credible plans to cause loss of
life have been disrupted . . . However, as the tragic attacks
of 7 July 2005 have shown, it is not possible to eliminate
completely the threat of terrorist attacks in this country.[18]

Such rare candour apart, the once-secret world of Whitehall
had really come in from the cold by the first decade of the
twenty-first century. In terms of detail and openness, the depic-
tion in the 2006 White Paper of the state apparatus for counter-
attacking the leading threat of the day would have inspired
disbelief in the Whitehall generation that drafted the 1957
Defence White Paper. Fifty years ago, for example, the peace-
time *existence* of the Secret Intelligence Service was not avowed;
the initials 'JIC', had they leaked, would have led to a serious
inquiry by the Joint Intelligence Committee and its staffs (which
were in the process of a reorganization in 1957, which was itself
top-secret); and the slightest whisper of what the Government

17 *Defence: Outline of Future Policy.*
18 *Countering International Terrorism*, p. 8.

Communications Headquarters did would very likely have led to a prosecution under Section 2 of the draconian Official Secrets Act, 1911 (now repealed). The 2006 White Paper, by contrast, gives a near-comprehensive account of the functioning of all the state's intelligence and security bodies including the cross-cutting Joint Terrorism Analysis Centre housed within the main building of the Security Service, MI5.

Openness about process and instruments is important, but first-order contrasts need to be assessed if other comparisons are to be set in proper context. Magnitude of threats is at the top of the list. For if one contemplates the worst that al-Qaeda and its imitators – or even an emerging rogue state with a chemical, biological, radiological or even nuclear capability – can do, it simply does not compare in impact or consequences to a thermonuclear attack on the United Kingdom of the kind the Soviet Union could have mounted in a few hours from the mid to late 1950s. Equally, the likelihood of such a Soviet attack was very small unless war came through catastrophic miscalculation or inadvertence.[19] Jihadist attacks, by contrast, were deemed inevitable *before* July 2005 and continue to be assessed as highly likely today and for a substantial period ahead. And as a senior Whitehall contingency planner put it in 2002: 'We did assume rationality with the Sovs. Now in Al Quaeda you have a bunch of people who just want to kill you ... and it doesn't matter what the target is and who gets in the way.'[20]

Given the continuity of the UK's non-partisan crown servants, many of the framers and constructors of the new protective state (including David Omand, Kevin Tebbit and Richard Mottram) were fully aware of the Whitehall esti-

---

19 See NA, PRO, CAB 158/47, JIC (62) 70, 'Escalation', 14 November 1962.
20 Quoted in Hennessy, *The Secret State*, p. 211.

mates of what hydrogen weapons on Britain would do to the kingdom in a few hours. They were equally aware of the physical and human wreckage likely to be left in the weeks, months and years that followed nuclear attack – what Edwin Muir, in his remarkable post-World War III ('The seven days war that put the world to sleep') poem, *The Horses*, described as

> That old bad world that swallowed its children quick
> At one great gulp.[21]

Muir, writing in the mid-1950s, expressed with his special Orcadian eloquence what his – and my – generation felt about living under the shade of the bomb. Eric Hobsbawm spoke for all of us when, recalling the 1950s in 2002, he said, '[i]t was a bad time . . . because we lived under the black shadow of the mushroom clouds . . . we were all living in a kind of nervous hysteria'.[22]

Looking back, 1954 was for 'that bad old world' what 2001 was for today's. It was the year in which not only Whitehall's scientists, intelligence analysts and planners realized just what a single H-bomb could do; the whole world took it on board, too, as Edwin Muir plainly did. The moment can be dated precisely – 31 March 1954 at a Presidential news conference in Washington. Eisenhower's special adviser on atomic weapons, Lewis Strauss, was there to reassure the American public about the Japanese fishermen contaminated by the most recent US H-bomb test in the Pacific. But, in reply to a simple question from a journalist, about the size and power of a

---

21   Edwin Muir, 'The Horses' in *One Foot in Eden* (London: Faber, 1956), pp. 73–4. I am very grateful to my friend Andy Dalton for bringing this poem to my attention.
22   Quoted in Peter Hennessy, *Having It So Good: Britain in the Fifties* (London: Allen Lane, The Penguin Press, 2006), p. 133.

thermonuclear weapon, he delivered a reply that was heard around the world:

> Strauss: '. . . in effect it can be made as large as you wish, as large as the military requirement demands, that is to say an H-bomb can be made as – large enough to take out a city.'
> Journalist: 'How big a city? Any city? New York?'
> Strauss: 'The metropolitan area, yes.'[23]

Within a few months the Churchill Cabinet had approved the manufacture of a British H-bomb.[24] And within a year of Strauss's statement, every member of the Cabinet was given a personal copy of the Strath Report on the effects of a thermonuclear attack on the UK.[25] The Strath group estimated that ten 10-megaton Soviet H-bombs dropped on the British Isles would kill 12 million people and seriously injure a further 4 million (nearly a third of the entire population) even before the fall-out spread its poison across the country. As to the impact on survivors, Strath told ministers:

> However successful the educative process might be, it would still be impossible to forecast how the nation would react to nuclear assault. The effect of this on dense populations would remain beyond the imagination until it happened. Whether this country could withstand an all-out attack and still be in any state to carry on hostilities must be very doubtful.[26]

---

23 Lorna Arnold, *Britain and the H-Bomb* (Basingstoke: Palgrave, 2001), p. 20.
24 NA, PRO, CAB 128/27, CC(54)53, 'Conclusions', 26 July 1954.
25 See Hennessy, *The Secret State*, pp. 121–46.
26 NA, PRO, CAB 134/940, HDC (55)3, 'The Defence Implications of Fall-Out from a Hydrogen Bomb: Report by a Group of Officials', 8 March 1955.

Five years later, another group of scientists and civil servants on the Joint Inter-Services Group for the Study of All-Out Warfare (JIGSAW) completed a series of assessments of the point at which British society post-nuclear attack might fall apart, defining 'breakdown' as happening 'when the government of a country is no longer able to ensure that its orders are carried out':

This state of affairs could come about through the breakdown of the machinery of control . . . through the mass of people becoming preoccupied with their own survival rather than the country's war effort and prepared to run the risk of being shot rather than to obey orders which would seem to them to involve unreasonable personal risk, in a word, through the breakdown of morale.[27]

Nothing in the worst possibilities considered by the Cabinet Office's Civil Contingencies Secretariat since its creation in July 2001[28] comes anywhere near to the cataclysms contemplated by the Strath or JIGSAW groups. But, as the 2006 White Paper admits,

[g]iven the vast range of potential terrorist attack scenarios, with a wide range of potential consequences, it is neither practicable nor prudent to plan for every scenario. Instead, planning seeks to build generic capabilities and plans, able to be drawn on flexibly in the response to a wide range of terrorist (and other) events.[29]

---

27   NA, PRO, DEFE 10/402, 'Study Group', 1960. SG (60)35, 'Note on the Concept and Definitions of Breakdown', Edgar Anstey, 10 June 1960.
28   *Countering International Terrorism*, p. 26.
29   *Ibid.*

Here, there exists a profound difference between Cold War post-attack capacity and today's capabilities in proportion to the threats faced. As Matthew Grant's research has shown, at no time between 1948, when a Civil Defence Bill was rushed through Parliament, and the fall of the Berlin Wall 41 years later, did Britain possess a home defence capacity anywhere near capable of coping with a nuclear attack.[30] Today, for the first time since VE Day in May 1945, the UK has a civil defence system that approaches a reality in terms of likely emergencies.

Whitehall's early-twenty-first-century review, which found statutory form in the Civil Contingencies Act 2004, examined the problem not just in terms of the impact of terrorist attacks but as an emergencies problem in the round embracing a wide range of factors – what before global warming used to be called 'acts of god' (such as floods); epidemics affecting humans or animals; the impact of small groups threatening parts of the so-called 'critical national infrastructure' (such as the fuel protestors in 2000); or industrial disputes that threaten the essentials of life. The 2004 Act swept up and revised existing emergency powers and civil defence legislation, fusing them, in a single statute, with the generic capabilities needed to deal with the consequences of a terrorist assault on people, infrastructure, essential services and systems.

Examples cited in the 2006 White Paper include the 7,000-plus police officers trained to deal with threats arising from chemical, biological, radiological or nuclear attack; investment in mass decontamination equipment; search and rescue and emergency water-pumping capabilities and the capacity to deploy them at national, regional and local levels.[31] The Civil

---

30   Matthew Grant, 'Civil Defence Policy in Cold War Britain, 1945–68', unpublished PhD thesis, Queen Mary, University of London, 2006.
31   *Countering International Terrorism*, p. 26.

Contingencies Act also gives the state huge, if temporary, powers to place its hands back on once-nationalized now-privatized utilities for the duration of a crisis. Here lies another significant difference between now and the high Cold War when gas, electricity and water were in all in state ownership.[32]

In his 'Securing Our Future' Lecture to the Royal United Services Institute on 13 February 2006, Gordon Brown, the Chancellor of the Exchequer, himself a historian by formation, drew his own comparisons between Cold War past and counter-terrorism present. He talked briefly about Cold War 'weapons that were military or intelligence based'.[33] As a practitioner-turned-scholar, Michael Herman put it:

> the Cold War was in a special sense an intelligence conflict . . . Never before in peacetime have the relationships of competing power blocks been so influenced by intelligence assessments. Never before have the collection of intelligence and its denial to the adversary been such central features of an international rivalry. The Cold War transformed intelligence into a major element of the peacetime international security system.[34]

Countering international terrorism, too, is crucially and substantially an intelligence-based activity, as can be seen from the 'CONTEST: Strategy and Delivery' and 'British Intelli-

---

32   *Ibid.*, pp. 24–6.
33   Gordon Brown, 'Securing Our Future', *RUSI Journal*, Vol. 151, No. 2, April 2006, p. 14.
34   Michael Herman, 'The Role of Military Intelligence Since 1945', paper delivered to the Twentieth Century British Politics and Administration Seminar at the Institute of Historical Research, University of London, 24 May 1989; I am very grateful to Mr Herman for sending me his latest thinking on this theme: Michael Herman, 'Intelligence in the Cold War: How Much Did it Matter? Some reflections', paper delivered in Oslo, 28 April–1 May 2005. Later published in Michael Herman, J. Kenneth McDonald and Vojtech Mastny, *Did Intelligence Matter in the Cold War?* (Norwegian Institute for Defence Studies, 2006), pp. 9–41.

gence Flows' charts on pages 27 and 31 (of which more in a moment). Like the Cold War in its day, countering terrorism absorbs a high proportion of the overall resources of the British intelligence community and dominates the setting of its priority targets.

But, naturally, there are important differences between the nature of the Cold War and the counter-terrorism intelligence efforts. Two in particular stand out. The Cold War intelligence attack was state-to-state. The counter-terrorism attack has a multiplicity of targets, some of which are states, but the most worrying single player of the early-twenty-first century – al-Qaeda – is a state of mind rather than a state; a source of inspiration and guidance through individuals and the internet, with followers and imitators across a large part of the globe in the form of loose networks or clusters of individuals.

The second profound difference lies in the realms of intelligence 'secrets and mysteries'. During the Cold War, 'secrets' embraced information which, through a mixture of open and clandestine sources, could be acquired with some accuracy for much of the time – the Warsaw Pact's order of battle; the location and capability of much of its weaponry (though intimate knowledge of Soviet missiles and the technology within them was often as vexing as it was vital, which is why Oleg Penkovsky was so important as an agent-in-place 1961–3).[35] The 'mysteries' were the intentions of the Soviet leadership. All the UK and NATO war-planning exercises began with a change of regime in Moscow to adventurous hard-liners as the event which triggered the escalation to all-out war and nuclear release with which they ended.[36]

---

35 Jerrold L. Schechter and Peter S. Deriabin, *The Spy Who Saved the World: How a Soviet Colonel Changed the Course of the Cold War* (London: Brassey's, 1995).

36 Hennessy, *The Secret State*, pp. 113–19; for the latest exercise to be declassified, WINTEX 75, see NA, PRO, CAB 134/3911.

Today the 'secrets and mysteries' equation is reversed. The intentions of al-Qaeda and its imitators are murderously plain. It's where its operatives are – in which European hotel room or British back-street – and with what device in their suitcase or rucksack that is the 'mystery'. Equally problematic in counter-intelligence terms is who and where are the inspirers, briefers and promoters of terrorist cells. Unlike the KGB or the GRU, they do not operate under 'legal' cover from embassies or trade missions in London. It is like dealing all the time with the Soviet 'illegals' who were extremely difficult to locate. And the internet gives inspirers, briefers and operators a fast, real-time communications capability that no side enjoyed at any stage of the Cold War.

The 'threat-from-within' element of the Cold War and counter-terrorism intelligence efforts makes for an especially fascinating and anxiety-inducing comparison. Surveillance techniques and equipment have advanced dramatically since high Cold War days, but the task of identifying home-grown jihadist terrorists remains acute. The degree of the problem was not fully appreciated by the secret world before the 7 July 2005 attacks in London and the White Paper a year later indicated that the watchers and the analysts were still in the process of catching up. After noting that '[a]s we saw in the tragic events of 7 July 2005, terrorists inspired by Islamist extremism may come from within British communities – the bombers were British citizens brought up in this country' and listing Libya, Algeria, Jordan, Saudi Arabia, Iraq and Somalia as the sources of 'terrorist suspects investigated in the UK', the document deals in an understated way with the surprise and the worry within the intelligence community of the magnitude of the domestic as well as the global problem by recognizing 'that the scale of the threat is potentially still increasing'.[37]

At the time the White Paper was published, it was estimated that

---

37   *Countering International Terrorism*, p. 8.

in the UK 1,200 people were actively involved in jihadist terrorist and terrorist-supporting activities. There were about 20 investigations under way into overlapping groups amounting to about 200 individuals. By the time Dame Eliza Manningham-Buller delivered her threat assessment to the Mile End Institute in November 2006, these figures had increased significantly (see pages 67–8). Distinguishing between helpers and operators – penumbra and core – was proving immensely difficult. By contrast, at the height of Provisional IRA activities in the early 1980s, British intelligence was confident in its estimates that the organization had around 10,000 sympathizers in Northern Ireland, 1,200 of whom were prepared to give support to around 600 active terrorists. The core and the periphery were much easier to distinguish and to measure in gauging the Northern Ireland-related terrorist threat than when countering today's Islamist terrorism.[38]

When comparisons are made with the 1940s, 1950s and 1960s threats, the nature of the domestic jihadist problem can prompt something of a 'you knew where you were with the Communist Party of Great Britain' reaction. There is something in it, and not simply the huge difference that the CPGB was a legitimate political party which stood peacefully for election and was in no way a terrorist organization. As Security Service files which reached the National Archives in the late 1990s and early 2000s indicate, the CPGB's headquarters in 16 King Street, Covent Garden and its telephones were bugged 24 hours a day.[39] Individual files for Party executive members and influential Party intellectuals such as Maurice Dobb in Cambridge show a close and persistent surveillance over decades, including the opening of mail and a watch on them when travelling abroad.[40] The bulk of it, including

---

38   Private information.
39   See, for example, NA, PRO, HO 45/25577, 25578, 25579, 'Disturbances: Communist Party of Great Britain: Report on Aims, Policy, Activities and Meetings, 1948–54'. Especially revealing are the Metropolitan Police Special Branch fortnightly summaries for MI5 and the Home Office.
40   NA, PRO, KV 2/1759, 'Dobb, Maurice Herbert', 1951–4.

Dobb's files, revealed no espionage or espionage-recruitment activity of any kind, even though, during his 1951–2 interrogation, the KGB agent within MI6, Kim Philby, said Dobb was the one of the few Communists he knew at Cambridge. He told his MI5 interrogator, William Skardon, on 28 December 1951 that Dobb, as a lecturer in the Cambridge Economics Faculty, 'made no attempt in the course of tutorials to proselytize him to the Communist dogma'[41] and, in later life, after defecting to Moscow, Philby would insist that his joining the Communist underground took place in Vienna, post-Cambridge. 'On my very last day at Cambridge,' Philby told his biographer Phillip Knightley,

> I decided that I would become a communist. I asked a don I admired, Maurice Dobb, how I should go about it. He gave me an introduction to a communist group in Paris, a perfectly legal and open group. They in turn passed me on to a communist underground organization in Vienna. Matters were at crisis point in Austria [in 1933–4] and this underground organization needed volunteers. I helped smuggle wanted socialists and communists out of the country.[42]

'Maurice Dobb in his tweed suit!' as a later non-Communist lecture attendee, and a future Labour father of the House of Commons, Tam Dalyell, remembers him,[43] absorbed a great deal of effort from MI5, those who opened his mail in the Cambridge GPO sorting office and the Cambridge City Police special branch officers who kept an eye on CPGB meetings in

---

41   *Ibid.*: 'Extract from an interview of H. A. R. Philby by W. J. Skardon on 28 December 1951'.
42   Phillip Knightley, *Philby: KGB Masterspy* (London: Andrew Deutsch, 1988), p. 36.
43   Conversation with Tam Dalyell, 13 August 2006.

the town; but, like most *overt* Party members, he was not an acute cause of anxiety. Naturally, it was the *covert* Party members and sympathizers in high places in British public service that most concerned the Security Service.

MI5, in fact, had a certain sympathy for the motivations of the openly active working-class members of the CPGB, however misguided they thought them to be. In an assessment of the threat posed by the CPGB prepared for Attlee and a small group of ministers in 1947–8, the Security Service said of the 45,000-strong Party that its membership fell

> into two distinct sections. By far the larger of these sections, consisting of the full-time executives and the working-class members, is mainly concerned with domestic policy: wages, housing, education, taxation, unemployment, health, pensions, and so on.[44]

MI5's analysts found that '[t]he most striking feature about the British Communist Party is that it is, first and foremost, a political party like other political parties. In so far as it partakes also of the character of a subversive or conspiratorial organization, it does so to a secondary degree.'[45]

It was the privileged intellectuals infused by Marxism–Leninism that seriously worried officers of the Security Service as they adapted to the long-term target in the developing Cold War. 'The smaller section,' they briefed the Labour ministers,

---

44   NA, PRO, CAB 130/37, 'The Communist Party. Its Strengths and Activities: Its Penetration of Government Organizations and of the Trade Unions', attached as an appendix to a report prepared by a Working Party on 'Security Measures Against Encroachments by Communists or Fascists in the United Kingdom' for ministers on GEN 226, The Cabinet Committee on European Policy, and circulated to them on 26 May 1948.
45   *Ibid.*

the intellectuals of the Party, comprising University students [a tiny proportion of the population in the late 1940s; a mere 74,764 students were attending British universities in 1947–8][46] and graduates, civil servants and members of the professions, is on the other hand primarily concerned with international issues and this is the interest which it has in common with the amorphous body of 'communist sympathizers', who are less sympathetic to the British Communist Party than to the ideological conception of international communism. If there were any subversive activity on behalf of a foreign power carried out in peace-time, one would expect it to be carried out by individuals of the intellectual group acting on their own initiative. The working-class group is unlikely to be the source of peace-time espionage.[47]

Stalin's clandestine 'intellectual' British helpers were most unlikely to be caught by the bugs in the walls at King Street, the tap on its phones or the MI5 team in Mount Pleasant sorting office in London with its room full of kettles steaming open the early-morning mail addressed to leading Party members in London.

A few years after the big MI5 assessment for Mr Attlee's team, a system of 'positive vetting', as opposed to a mere 'negative' checking of the MI5 and Special Branch files (MI5 alone in the late 1940s kept 250,000 files on members 'of the Communist Party and its fellow travellers')[48] was being constructed for the thousand or so public servants thought likely to cause serious harm to British interests if they moonlighted

---

46   Peter Hennessy, *Never Again: Britain 1945–51* (London: Cape, 1992), p. 161.
47   NA, PRO, CAB 130/37, 'The Communist Party'.
48   NA, PRO, CAB 120/30, PV(50)11, 'Committee on Positive Vetting. Report', 27 October 1950.

for the KGB or the GRU (the vetting net stretched eventually to cover nearly 70,000 crown servants and military by the early 1980s). Even the positive vetting of an official's background, private life and social contacts would not, the system's framers rightly thought, uncover the most dangerous and deeply concealed of Stalin's Brits. Such inquiries, the Committee on Positive Vetting told ministers in autumn 1950,

> will fail to detect the really dangerous crypto-communist. The latter's true nature will not be revealed by his accomplices and is unlikely to be known to his ordinary acquaintances. The detection of such persons can only be secured by the scientifically planned study of Communist activities which it is the task of the Security Authorities to carry out.[49]

This was almost certainly a disguised reference to the so-called VENONA decrypts which American and British codebreakers worked on from late 1946 (after GRU encrypters in New York had given them a break by sloppily re-using one-time pads).

By 1950, this cryptographic attack had led to the uncovering of the atomic spy Klaus Fuchs, and, a year later, it would expose the diplomat Donald Maclean.[50] Failing a signals intelligence breakthrough, only a high-level defector could give British Intelligence a chance of uncovering the concealed and the dangerous.

Until the late 1960s and early 1970s, when a scattering of Trotskyite and Maoist groups came under MI5 surveillance and caused the Joint Intelligence Committee concern lest they

---

49   *Ibid.*
50   For the impact of VENONA see Christopher Andrew, 'The Venona Secret' in K. G. Robertson (ed.), *War, Resistance and Intelligence: Essays in Honour of M. R. D. Foot* (London: Pen and Sword, 1999), pp. 203–26.

should interfere with military and civil defence preparations in a period of rising international East/West tension that might lead to war,[51] the CPGB and the clandestine Communists were the chief concern of British counter-intelligence. By the mid-1950s, the JIC was confident that by the time a third world war broke out, 'the whole known organization of the British Communist Party will have been smashed. Even if a secret and unknown party organization were in existence at the time, and we consider this unlikely, it would not devote itself to the task of organizing sabotage.'[52]

The CPGB was well organized and hierarchical. Penetrating it was relatively straightforward: there were known buildings to be bugged, phone-lines to be tapped and meetings to be infiltrated; the Security Service did a nice line, too, in 'turning' the membership secretaries of various Party branches and front organizations.[53] Communists and Communist sympathizers had an ideology which, for many, amounted to a secular religion and, in their eyes, several beacon societies existed east of the Elbe and, from 1949, in China. Until the Soviet suppression of the Hungarian uprising in 1956, the CPGB was a near monolith on the far Left[54] – and, because of its taking the Soviet line, a substantial, but by no means insuperable intelligence problem.

---

51   NA, PRO, CAB 186/8, Part 2, JIC(A)(71)16, 'The security of the United Kingdom Base in a situation Leading to a Threat of General War; Annex: Subversive Organizations in the United Kingdom'.
52   NA, PRO, CAB 158/24, JIC(56)41, 'Likely Scale and Nature of an Attack on the United Kingdom in a Global War up to 1960', 10 May 1956.
53   Private information.
54   The Trotskyist Revolutionary Communist Party, later the Revolutionary Socialist League, was scarcely a rival until it transformed itself into Militant Tendency in the mid-1960s and began to operate inside the Labour Party until, with great difficulty, Neil Kinnock succeeded in marginalizing it 20 years later. (See *The Times* obituary of its leading light, Ted Grant, 26 July 2006).

When contemplating early-twenty-first century UK-based targets, it's not surprising that a 'Those were the days' reaction is what one gets if one turns the subject back to Cold War operations in conversation with the more seasoned of the Queen's secret servants. Watching Stalin's, Khrushchev's or Brezhnev's Brits was a painstaking, sloggy business. But, except in the last days of peace before a third world war, there was no real likelihood of them turning to violence. As the JIC's 1956 assessment put it, '[o]rganized sabotage before war is most unlikely because the Soviet leaders will be unwilling to give away their plans to Communists in the United Kingdom'.[55]

As we have seen, the plan was to 'smash' the capacity of organized domestic Communists, open and secret members alike, in the run-up to war. By the early to mid-1950s an elaborate MI5–Home Office plan, codenamed HILLARY, existed for a substantial round-up and detention of possible subversives and saboteurs. It embraced 3,000 people in all: 1,000 would be British subjects (including about 200 women); 2,000 would be aliens (of whom 500 were women). Those British males earmarked for detention who lived in England south of a line from the Severn to the Wash would be kept initially on Epsom Racecourse in Surrey; northerners would be taken to a holiday camp in Rhyl, North Wales. Southern-based aliens would go to Ascot Racecourse in Berkshire; northern aliens to Rhyl. The women would be sent to Holloway Gaol or to an unspecified prison in the north. Once processed they were, wartime conditions permitting, to be fully interned in various holiday camps on the Isle of Man.[56]

---

55   NA, PRO, CAB 158/24, JIC(56)41.
56   NA, PRO, KV 4/225, 'Policy: Setting up of Detention Camps in the UK for the Detention of British Subjects and the Internment of Aliens in the Event of an Emergency, 1948–1954', 'Internment Camps in War. Summary of Agreed Plans as 9 February 1954'.

Today's equivalent is greatly more alarming. The possibility of a serious, violent assault by jihadist terrorists somewhere in the UK is real and constant. In these terms, the greatest difference between Cold War surveillance of the domestic threat and that of the twenty-first century is the day-in, day-out 24-hour watch kept by the Joint Terrorism Analysis Centre, which processes an average of around 1,000 separate items of intelligence each week, many of which require instant analysis and rapid decisions taken on the risk assessment based on that analysis.[57]

Another difference of considerable concern is the sources of motivation. It was relatively simple for the Cold War secret state and those who oversaw and staffed it to understand, even with a dash of sympathy, what led to the recruitment and inspiration of UK Communists.[58] Post-9/11 Whitehall has found this one of its most vexing problems in terms of the sometimes swift transition of individuals from concern to anger through charitable or financial support for terrorist groups to being prepared to carry out a terrorist act themselves.[59]

---

57   See 'Cats' Eyes in the Dark', *The Economist*, 19–25 March 2005, p. 83.

58   Herbert Morrison as Labour Home Secretary within the World War II coalition alluded to the well-springs of Communist Party recruitment in a letter to Churchill in November 1943 when the War Cabinet considered the danger of Soviet espionage continuing (as indeed it did) when the UK and the USSR were allies. 'In order', he wrote, '. . . to do anything effective in the way of stopping the risk of leakage it would be necessary (a) to bring it home to the Communist Party that their espionage activities do not pay and are likely to discredit the Party, and (b) to make it clear to all Government servants – *including those who are attracted to the Communist doctrines by a creditable zeal for social reform* [my italics] – that loyalty to the Communist Party stands on a different footing from loyalty to any other political party because loyalty to the Communist Party may entail disloyalty to the state.' NA, PRO, KV 4/251, 'Morrison to Churchill', 9 November 1943.

59   See the 'How Does Radicalization Occur?' section of *Countering International Terrorism*, p. 10.

How helpful, in those terms, are past counter-terrorist operations? Britain's long experience with trying to understand and thwart Northern Ireland-related terrorism was of limited use except for the surveillance techniques developed to counter it which are of enduring value. For not only were the well-springs of violence different in kind, Provisional IRA active service units did not see it as a step closer to paradise to go up with their own bombs. Also they worked for a tightly run, hierarchical organization which could be – and was – penetrated by British intelligence. The PIRA threat, too, was a domestic problem with international implications, and the terrorists' purpose was to use violence as part of a strategy to negotiate the British out of Northern Ireland. The al-Qaeda breed of threat is an international problem with domestic implications, and the violence is the end itself; there is no negotiating strategy.[60]

Even the Whitehall assessments of Middle East-generated terrorism in the mid-1970s are of limited applicability to today's threats. For example, the Petersen Report prepared for the Ministerial Committee on Terrorism in March 1975 concentrated almost exclusively on the handling of aircraft hijacking after a spate of such incidents involving British aircraft at home and abroad.[61] Amid the improvements suggested for command-and-control during such crises and the difficulties surrounding the despatch of the Special Air Service PAGODA troop to incidents abroad, some attention was given to the psychology of Middle East-related terrorism. But this was

---

60   I owe this thought to a senior military figure with direct experience of countering both Northern Ireland-related terrorism and that of al-Qaeda and its imitators. See Major-General Jonathan Shaw, 'The Long War: A Manifesto for Victory', paper prepared for the Royal College of Defence Studies, July 2006.

61   NA, PRO, CAB 134/3973, TM (75)1, 'Counter-Terrorist Arrangements: Memorandum by the Chairman of the Official Committee', 4 March 1975.

limited to the handling of crises, not the mentalities that generated the action in the first place. 'Experience has shown',
the Petersen group[62] told ministers, 'that the success of an
operation can depend critically on an accurate assessment of
the terrorists' mood and their likely reactions to police
activity or proposals. In some cases a psychologist/psychia-
trist might be able to make a major contribution to such an
assessment.'[63]

In fact, the Cabinet Office has been continuously servicing
committees on terrorism of one kind or another for nearly 40
years since the Northern Ireland 'Troubles' re-erupted in the
late 1960s and Harold Wilson created MISC 238, under his
own chairmanship, in February 1969.[64] Every prime minister
since has had a Cabinet committee on Northern Ireland[65] and
Mr Blair's is still in existence. But the past five years have seen
a qualitative and a quantitative leap in terrorist-related
machinery of government, though, understandably enough, it
is still small compared to the proportion of the elaborate
Cabinet committee structure devoted to Cold War purposes, as
the swiftest glance at a 1960s Cabinet Secretary's 'Committee
Organization Book' will attest.[66]

It is divided into two modes – planning and operations –
and its structures reflect the four 'P's (prevention, pursuit,
protection and preparation) that are at the heart of the Government's counter-terrorism strategy, or CONTEST.[67] It has
gone through a few refinements and mutations over the past

---

62   Sir Arthur Petersen was Permanent Secretary at the Home Office.
63   *Ibid.*
64   NA, PRO, CAB 130/416, MISC 238(69), 1st meeting, 26 February
1969.
65   See Peter Hennessy, *The Prime Minister*, pp. 346–7, 372, 457, 501–2.
66   See, for example, NA, PRO, CAB 161/13, 'Cabinet Office: Committee
Organization Book, 1963'.
67   *Countering International Terrorism*, p. 9.

five years, but currently (2006) the 'Strategy and Delivery' structure looks like that shown in Figure 1.1.[68]

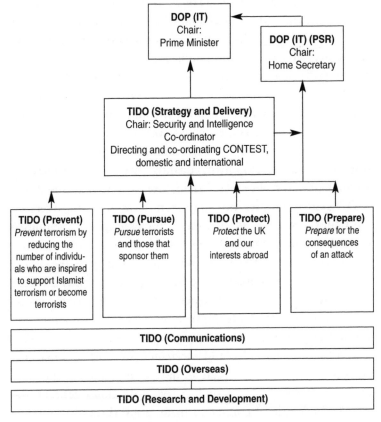

Figure 1.1   CONTEST: Strategy and delivery

---

68   This and the two organograms that follow were prepared initially by the author and Sir David Omand, when Co-ordinator of Security and Intelligence, and updated in early 2006 by the Cabinet Office before Sir Richard Mottram and the author addressed a seminar at the National Liberal Club in London on 8 February 2006 organized jointly by the *Guardian* and the First Division Association of Civil Servants. The original organograms were published in *RUSI Journal*, Vol. 150, No. 3 (June 2003) to accompany papers by Omand and Hennessy. The original 'British Intelligence Flows' diagram accompanied 'Cats' Eyes in the Dark' in *The Economist*, 19–25 March 2005.

The system is overseen by a sub-committee of the Cabinet's Defence and Overseas Policy Committee known as DOP(IT), i.e. Defence and Overseas Policy (International Terrorism), which the Prime Minister chairs. Much of the detailed work is undertaken by DOP(IT) (PSR – Protection, Security and Resilience) chaired by the Home Secretary. Beneath the two ministerially led committees is the so-called TIDO machine (TIDO indicating Terrorism International Defence and Overseas) staffed by civil servants, the intelligence community and the military. As well as groups reflecting the four 'P's, there are three cross-cutting TIDOs for communications, overseas, and research and development, dealing with counter-terrorist equipment and techniques. When, after a serious incident, the TIDO system mutates into an operations mode,[69] it is overseen by COBR (known as 'Cobra'), the emergency committee housed in the Cabinet Office Briefing Room (itself an early 1970s creation of the Cold War co-located with the Prime Minister's 'Nuclear Release Room').[70] COBR acts as a mixed committee (its composition depends on the nature of the crisis) and, when ministers are present, it is chaired by either the Prime Minister or the Home Secretary. As Figure 1.2 indicates, it is linked televisually and electronically with comparable emergency rooms in the regions, and, if necessary, in the UK's military districts. The conduct of operations reflects the standard cascade of command from 'gold' through 'silver' to 'bronze'.

---

69   As it did in the small hours of 10 August 2006 as 23 arrests were being made of those suspected of preparing to down ten transatlantic airliners. (See Philip Webster, Sean O'Neill and Stewart Tendler, 'A plan "to commit unimaginable mass murder"', *The Times*, 11 August 2006.)

70   NA, PRO, HO 223/129, GEN 8(71)1 (Final), 'Crisis Management Working Party. Costed Proposals for the Whitehall Situation Centre', 1 July 1971.

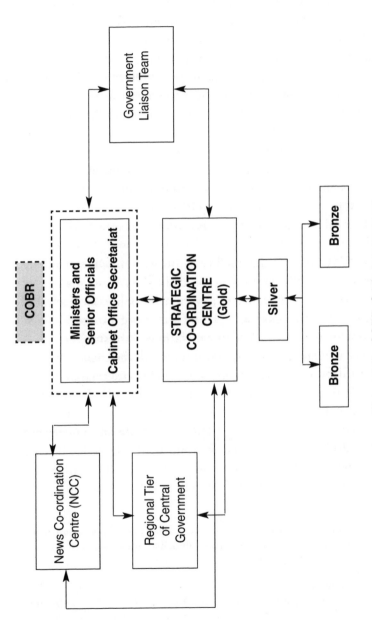

Figure 1.2 COBR: Crisis management

The intelligence flow diagram (Figure 1.3) is largely self-explanatory. JTAC, now some 120-strong and made up of officials seconded from the secret agencies, Whitehall, the military and the police, is responsible for the UK's 'Threat Levels' alert system which was made public in July 2006 as it reflects international terrorism. 'Irish and other domestic terrorism' is assessed by the Security Service, MI5.[71] There are five threat levels:

Low	an attack is unlikely;
Moderate	an attack is possible, but not likely;
Substantial	an attack is a strong possibility;
Severe	an attack is highly likely;
Critical	an attack is expected imminently.[72]

If JTAC believes the intelligence so warrants, it can swiftly trigger a COBR meeting if needed. JTAC also distributes warnings to a wide range of government, police, local authority, military, transport and private sector organizations which deal with aspects of the 'Critical National Infrastructure'.[73]

The diagram also incorporates several of the changes recommended by the Butler inquiry into intelligence relating to the Iraq War of 2003, most notably the creation of a Professional Head of Intelligence Analysis.[74] It also captures the fusing of the functions of the Cabinet Office's Security and Intelligence Co-ordinator with the chairmanship of the Joint Intelligence Committee, which occurred in November 2005 when Sir Richards Mottram replaced Bill Jeffrey as Co-ordinator.

---

71   *Threat Levels: The System to Assess the Threat from International Terrorism* (London: Stationery Office, July 2006). Introduction by Dr John Reid, Home Secretary, p. 1.
72   *Ibid.*, p. 2.
73   *Ibid.*, p. 3.
74   *Review of Intelligence on Weapons of Mass Destruction: Report of a Committee of Privy Counsellors*, HC898 (London: Stationery Office, July 2004).

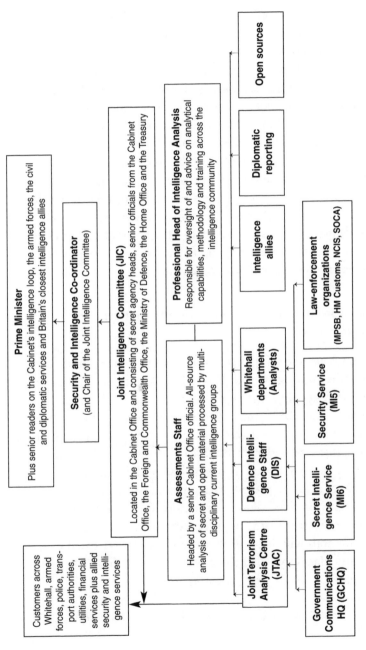

Figure 1.3 Britain's intelligence flows

Tracing the reconfiguration of the state's counter-terrorist apparatus and listing the fistful of new counter-terrorist laws such as the Prevention of Terrorism Act 2005, the Terrorism Act 2006 and the Civil Contingencies legislation of 2004, as well as the relevant sections of the Immigration, Asylum and Nationality Act 2006, is relatively straightforward. Assessing the cumulative impact of the new home-grown as well as inter-national threats, the new state capabilities and the swathe of fresh legislation designed to combat them upon the nature of early-twenty-first-century British society, is altogether tougher. The initial response phase has seen a rush of related develop-ments and it is still early days in terms of appreciating its significance. But, as in the Cold War, current anxieties and perilous possibilities are going to be a decades-long problem, and early assessments have to be made.

The protective state and early-twenty-first-century British society

Many people of many nations were brave under the bombs [during World War II]. I doubt that the most important thing was Dunkirk or the Battle of Britain . . . I am persuaded that the most important thing that happened in Britain was that this nation chose to win or lose this war under the established rules of parliamentary procedure. It feared Nazism, but it did not choose to imitate it . . . Representative government, equality before the law, survived. Future generations who bother to read the official record of proceedings in the House of Commons will discover that British armies retreated from many places, but that there was no retreat from the prin-ciples for which your ancestors fought.[75]

---

75   Edward R. Murrow, 'A Reporter Remembers', *The Listener*, 28 Feb-ruary 1946.

In the aftermath of the July 2005 bombings, the Prime Minister, Tony Blair, during his regular monthly press briefing on 5 August, said in his opening statement: 'Let no one be in any doubt, the rules of the game are changing.' He went on to list a 12-point plan to illustrate the shift.[76] In one sense, the 'rules' tend to change both literally and in terms of states of mind after an atrocity which seriously alters existing appreciations and expectations that affect the norms and the nature of society thereafter.

This was certainly true of the Birmingham bombing carried out by the Provisional IRA on 21 November 1974, in which 24 people died and nearly 200 were injured. As the Home Secretary, Roy Jenkins, who rushed a Prevention of Terrorism Bill through Parliament in the days that followed, put it, the bombs in the two city-centre pubs represented 'a different order of casualties from anything we had previously known'.[77] Jenkins was no lover of hurried law-making. But he quickly decided 'that the time had come to introduce this legislation, influenced alike by the desire to give reassurance to the country and by the belief that its provisions, which had now become acceptable although they would not hitherto have been so, would be of considerable and practical anti-terrorist utility.'[78] It was, in fact, less rushed than it appeared as, in Jenkins' words,

> We had carefully prepared contingency plans. These were made up of one measure which was for show and three which were of real practical importance. The first related to making the IRA an illegal organization in Great Britain. When I came back into office [in March 1974] I inherited from the outgoing Conservative Administration

---

76 'PM's Press Conference – 5 August 2005', www.direct.gov.uk.
77 Roy Jenkins, *A Life at the Centre* (London: Macmillan, 1991), p. 393.
78 *Ibid.*, p. 395

the view that this would be a mixture of the fruitless and the harmful. This view was lukewarmly supported by the police, who thought that driving the IRA underground might make it more difficult to penetrate.[79]

Jenkins, on 'that fraught November evening' changed his mind as 'I decided that the IRA's continued legal existence . . . had become an intolerable affront to the British people . . .'.[80]

He regarded the three 'practical' provisions as of much greater importance:

> The first empowered the police to detain terrorist suspects without having to formulate charges for forty-eight hours on their own authority, and then for another five days, provided they sought authority from a minister of the Crown in each case. The second introduced much tighter physical controls at the points of entry into Great Britain from both the north and south parts of Ireland. The third, which was the most controversial, enabled the Home Secretary to exclude from Great Britain citizens of the Republic of Ireland where it appeared to him, on advice, that they were involved or likely to be involved in acts of terrorism. This was drastic, particularly in relation to those from Northern Ireland, who of course held United Kingdom passports.[81]

The Jenkins Act endured across Labour and Conservative administrations alike and enjoyed a high level of cross-party and public consensus. Future atrocities (of which there were many) did not lead to a cataract of legislation. For example, as

---

79　*Ibid.*, pp. 393–4.
80　*Ibid.*, p. 394.
81　*Ibid.*

Simon Jenkins noted, it was greatly to Margaret Thatcher's credit that she did not rush to legislate after the Brighton bomb of 12 October 1984 which was intended to kill her and the bulk of her Cabinet.[82]

The early twenty-first century, by contrast, *did* see a cataract of terrorist and terrorist-related law-making. The Terrorism Act 2000 consolidated existing legislation and extended it to all forms of terrorism, not just Irish-related.[83] The very substantial Anti-Terrorism, Crime and Security Act 2001 was passed swiftly by Parliament in the wake of 9/11. It dealt with the freezing of assets belonging to terrorist organizations and, most controversially, allowed for the indefinite detention of foreign terrorist suspects, certified by the Secretary of State (i.e. the Home Secretary) as a threat to security, who could not be deported as they would likely suffer torture if returned to their country of origin. This section of the Act required the UK to derogate from the European Convention on Human Rights. It was overturned by the House of Lords in December 2004 as incompatible with the Convention.[84] As a consequence of this, the Blair Government drafted what became the Prevention of Terrorism Act 2005 enabling the Secretary of State 'to make a "non-derogating" control order against an individual who he has reasonable grounds for suspecting is involved in terrorism-related activity and where he considers it necessary for the protection of the public'.[85] The Terrorism Act 2006 extended the period for which a suspect can be detained without charge from 14 to 28 days (the Government wanted 90 days initially but could not command a majority for it in the House of

---

82 Simon Jenkins, *Thatcher and Sons: A Revolution in Three Acts* (London: Allen Lane, The Penguin Press, 2006), p. 101.
83 Andrew Blick and Stuart Weir, *The Rules of the Game* (Colchester: Democratic Audit, 2005), p. 8.
84 *Ibid.*, p. 9.
85 *Countering International Terrorism*, p. 19.

Commons). This last statute became mired in what Conor Gearty has called 'the politics of both the last atrocity and of the atrocity still to come'[86] and saw a lack of consensus between the political parties that was in stark contrast to the Jenkins legislation a generation earlier.

As Ed Murrow indicated to his BBC radio audience in 1946, the test of an open society under duress is the degree to which it does *not* tamper with liberty and due process in periods of great anxiety. To that extent 'the rules of the game' do not change. Sustaining the essentials of an open society remains a primary duty of government in a democracy. As Richard Mottram emphasizes in Chapter 2, the 'aim of Government policy, whether in countering international terrorism or responding to a range of other contingencies, is "to reduce the risk, so that people can go about their daily lives freely and with confidence"'.

To a remarkable degree this happened, certainly in mainland Britain, throughout the bulk of the Provisional IRA campaign. It was true, too, of the domestic side of the Cold War. For example, a purge of Communists and Communist sympathizers in the crown services did take place. But there was no naming and shaming of the kind that occurred in the United States in the 1940s and 1950s.[87] Wherever possible, alternative work was found for the purgees in non-sensitive areas of the public service. 'The idea was to keep them away from classified information and then they got on with their lives. We kept them away from the controls and that was it', as an intelligence community veteran put it.[88] For an open society the ambition, now as in the 1940s and 1950s and during the long IRA campaign, has to be to tighten up the necessary procedures without coarsening due process.

---

86 Conor Gearty, 'Beware Atrocity Politics', *The Tablet*, 16 July 2005.
87 David Caute, *The Great Fear: The Anti-Communist Purge under Truman and Eisenhower* (London: Secker and Warburg, 1978).
88 Private information. See also Hennessy, *The Secret State*, p. 97.

But it must be recognized that domestic jihadist terrorism is an especially vexing and tough problem to deal with in terms of the 'prevent' category of the quartet of 'P's. It was apparent from the *Report of the Official Account of the Bombings in London on 7th July 2005* that in the cases of the 'largely unexceptional' lives of three of the four men involved, '[l]ittle distinguishes their formative experiences from those of many others of the same generation, ethnic origin and social background . . .'[89] This was profoundly worrying to the security authorities. It led them to conclude that from 2001 to 2005 they had been largely firefighting – concentrating their resources on those most likely to assist in or carry out a terrorist act. As late as the spring of 2005, the best estimate was that the UK's home jihadist penumbra of serious sympathizers was around 2,000 people; the inner penumbra of those willing to give active help to terrorists or who might be prepared to commit a terrorist act themselves was around 200, and that, at any one time, about 20 individuals were on the streets capable of and willing to carry out an attack.[90]

After the bombings of 7 July 2005, a far more detailed and widespread 'richer picture' was required and sought to depict more accurately the magnitude of the problem and to enable the security authorities to penetrate much earlier the life-cycle of a potential terrorist. The fluidity between inner penumbra and the terrorist operatives has been recognized. And the latest estimate at the time the 2006 White Paper was published indicated that about 1,200 individuals were actively involved and merited serious investigation. It remained difficult, however, to distinguish between the rim of the inner penumbra and the active core.[91]

---

89 *Report of the Official Account of the Bombings in London on 7th July 2005*, HC1087 (London: Stationery Office, May 2006), p. 13.
90 Private information.
91 Private information.

The Populus survey for ITV News and *The Times* in July 2006 indicated that while 56 per cent of the 1.6 million Muslim community in the UK believed that the British Government was not doing enough to combat extremism and 50 per cent thought British intelligence had the right to infiltrate Muslim organizations, 13 per cent of those polled saw the four perpetrators of the 7 July bombings as 'martyrs' (with 7 per cent agreeing that suicide attacks on British civilians could be justified in some circumstances).[92] These figures suggest that a sizeable body of support exists within the British Muslim community and that the problem is of a kind and a magnitude never experienced before by the British intelligence community.

The *modus operandi* of the terrorist groupings adds to the concern. For example, the Provisional IRA would, as a first step, mount a detailed reconnaissance of a British target. The active service unit in Northern Ireland or the Republic would examine the reports of the recce team meticulously before choosing routes to the UK, safe houses, storage of equipment and timing of the operation itself with immense care. The slightest suspicion of something out of the ordinary, and the active service unit would call it off and go home.[93]

Al-Qaeda sympathizers are much more serendipitous. Much of their technical knowledge is transmitted over the internet. Once the equipment has been acquired, these loose networks think through what to do with it. If one target ceases to be viable, they quickly turn to another which promises to yield substantial casualties. If the operation is threatened, they are as likely to speed it up as to abandon it. This, too, presents a threat of a kind not faced before.[94] Combating it requires earlier and more intense surveillance. And it has led to a much

---

92 'Muslim Britain Split over "Martyrs" of 7/7', *The Times*, 4 July 2006.
93 Private information.
94 Private information.

greater MI5 presence across the country, with eight regional offices operating nationwide.

Thanks to the long IRA campaign, the UK was a CCTV'd nation long before 9/11. One unplanned benefit of the research and development programme stimulated by the 'Troubles' which led to the use of the 'automatic number plate reader' in Northern Ireland was the relative ease with which the London Congestion Charge equipment was installed. It was an IT program that had been thoroughly tested in advance. Indeed, the stimulus the IRA had given to surveillance techniques generally has proved of great value in combating jihadist terrorism. But it does not offer a way of ending it. For the 'prevent' section of the strategy requires the alteration of not just opinions and attitudes among the sympathetic penumbra but their most profound values as well, and the way the relationships between the Muslim and the non-Muslim worlds are perceived.[95]

The new protective state has made strenuous efforts both to understand the behavioural aspects of radicalization and to run 'roadshows' in which Muslim scholars take on arguments for extremist terrorism. Forums have been established to tackle the growth of Islamophobia in the UK and to engage with the Mosques and Imams National Advisory Board.[96] It is difficult, too, for the government of an increasingly secular state to preach back either in the form of an established national religion (not that such a tactic would help much, if at all) or a largely agreed version of national history and culture of the kind that existed in Macaulay's nineteenth century or even the early and mid-twentieth century of G. M. Trevelyan.[97]

---

95   I am grateful to Sir Robert Worcester of IPSOS MORI for the importance of distinguishing between opinions, attitudes and values. See his 'Powerful Tools to Assess People's Values', *Profile* 55, June/July 2006, www.profile-extra.co.uk.
96   *Countering International Terrorism*, p. 14.
97   See Stefan Collini, 'Writing "The National History"' in his *English Pasts: Essays in History and Culture* (Oxford: OUP, 1999), pp. 27–8.

The virtues and principles of the open society have multiple manifestations in early-twenty-first-century Britain. But the nature of that society and its secularity makes it hard for many in the UK to understand that, as Gellner put it, the Islamic world is a 'marked exception' from the general rule that 'in industrial or industrializing societies religion loses much of its erstwhile hold over men and society'. Over the past 100 years, Gellner wrote in the early 1990s,

> [t]he hold of Islam over the populations of the lands in which it is the main religion has in no way diminished . . . In some ways it has been markedly strengthened. Moreover, the hold is not restricted to certain layers of society . . . Its hold is as strong among ruling and urban classes and cultural elites as it is among less favoured sections of the population. It is as marked among traditionalist regimes as it is among those committed to social radicalism.[98]

Added to this lack of comprehension between religiously infused and secular-driven societies is the fact that *years* of careful cultural *rapprochement* and reasonable, sensitive official initiatives at home and abroad can be undone in *days* by events on the ground in the Middle East.

It is impossible to calibrate, let alone control, the ebb and flow of action/reaction on a national or an international basis. The sole certainty is that coping with the new forms of international terrorism will be a difficult and a protracted problem. In its acute form, it may not match or surpass the 40-plus years of Cold War containment or the near 30 years of countering Irish terrorism after 1968, but it could well do so. It will

---

98   Gellner, *Conditions of Liberty*, p. 15.

be a long-haul activity and an expensive one. The effects of the 'anaesthetic' are lifting. And it's becoming increasingly plain that the new protective state is already a considerable enterprise and that it doesn't come cheap. As the Chancellor of the Exchequer, Gordon Brown, told his Royal United Services Institute (RUSI) audience in February 2006, that by 2008 the country's aggregate investment in counter-terrorism will reach £2 billion a year, 'twice what we did before 11 September'. The staff complement of MI5 will have nearly doubled over the same period.[99] All the secret agencies have reordered their priorities to reflect the rise of jihadist international terrorism. And the nature of the threat it poses has led to collaborative working patterns of a closeness that surpasses Cold War and IRA days. As one senior intelligence figure put it, 'The community has come together because abroad has come home.'[100]

Abroad-coming-home has – and will – stretch the open society in the UK in a way it has never been tested before. The liberty/coercion equation will be at the heart of every element of the counter-terrorist strategy, especially in the days after an atrocity. But the criterion for the new protective state, like the World War II one and the Cold War version which followed, will be Karl Popper's (as outlined in his *The Open Society and Its Enemies* in 1945). 'We must', Popper wrote, 'plan for freedom and not only for security, if for no other reason than that only freedom can make security secure.'[101]

99   Gordon Brown, 'Securing Our Future', p. 15.
100 'Cats' Eyes in the Dark', p. 32
101 K. R. Popper, *The Open Society and Its Enemies: Volume II, The High Tide of Prophecy: Hegel, Marx and the Aftermath* (London: Routledge and Kegan Paul, 1945), p. 194.

2

Protecting the Citizen in the Twenty-first Century: Issues and Challenges

Richard Mottram

Introduction

Since the end of World War II, protection of the civilian population in the United Kingdom has often been the poor relation in UK government policy and expenditure priorities – indeed sometimes the relation best not mentioned. In the Cold War period, the scale of the prospective casualties should deterrence fail – not surprisingly – overwhelmed politicians and planners alike. Attempts to argue that civil defence had a place alongside UK nuclear weapons as part of a coherent strategy risked a rejoinder that such an approach was to contemplate nuclear war fighting.[1] Efforts to prepare the public to cope in the event of nuclear war – for example, in the pamphlet *Protect and Survive* – produced a counter-blast from supporters of nuclear disarmament as well as a superbly drawn and affecting cartoon book by Raymond Briggs.[2]

For a period this was the stuff of high politics – in 1983, for example, seen as perhaps of General Election-influencing scale – as well as of detailed and not necessarily so exciting planning

1   See, for example, E. P. Thompson, chapter 1 in E. P. Thompson and D. T. Smith, *Protest and Survive* (London: Penguin, 1980). The chapter critiques a letter from Professor Michael Howard on 'Reviving Civil Defence'.
2   R. Briggs, *When the Wind Blows* (London: Hamish Hamilton, 1982) .

and execution. Until the end of the Cold War, civil protection in the UK stood on two unequal legs. The first and largest was civil defence.[3] The second, most commonly referred to as 'civil emergency planning', covered work on plans and capabilities to secure the safety of the public in a range of (essentially local) emergencies short of war. With the end of the Cold War, the first leg soon withered. The emphasis fell quickly onto the second. This shift was reflected in the residual actions of central government, which quickly became restricted to the provision of brief best-practice guidance[4] and very limited sums of public expenditure.

As I shall briefly set out, the UK Government has learned, through somewhat bitter experience, that these arrangements were not fit to handle the civil protection challenges of the post-Cold War world. While these new arrangements were under development, many countries, including the UK, have faced an increasing threat from international terrorism. The UK's strategy for tackling this threat draws on these wider civil protection arrangements.[5]

---

3   *The Establishment of Arrangements Relating to the Organisation and Protection of the Civil Population in Response to a Hostile Attack by a Foreign Power* (UK Civil Defence Act 1948, Section 9(1)).

4   Extant guidance at that time amounted to some 30 pages in all.

5   Civil protection is defined as being 'about protecting the public from the effects of emergencies (whatever their causes may be). In addition to risk assessment and planning, it includes taking action before an emergency to mitigate its possible effects and responding in such a way that minimizes the impact of the emergency on the public and speeds recovery from that impact. In the case of terrorist attack, civil protection does not include action by the intelligence services or the police to prevent an attack from occurring or apprehending those involved (whether before, during or after the attack). Civil protection does include, however, protecting the public from the consequences of such an attack. In the case of a terrorist bomb, dealing with the effects and aftermath of the bomb would be regarded as civil protection': *The Future of Emergency Planning in England and Wales – A Discussion Document* (Cabinet Office, 2001).

Along the way there has been a fundamental shift in the purpose and organization of civil protection in the UK. Out has gone the remains of the Cold War model of civil defence focused on a single, monolithic, external threat, managed top-down by central government in secret and restricted to a small, mainly public-sector community. In its place has come a model better suited to a modern 'network society',[6] with its increased connections and interdependencies bringing with them greater vulnerability to external shock. The characteristics of this model are very different. It has to address a wide range of risks. As a result, it involves a broad range of actors, in the public sector and beyond. The need for secrecy is much reduced. Most significantly, work at local level is the building block of preparedness. The scale of this shift has been characterized as moving from the 'secret state' to the 'protecting or protective state'.[7]

Post-Cold War challenges: the three 'F's

Much of what had been used for civil defence was clearly life-expired. But, while everyone was relieved to be rid of the obviously superfluous *physical* infrastructure of civil defence, the decision by governments during the 1990s to retreat from their role as far as possible rather than update it to the needs of a modern networked society left three key organizational gaps. First, the opportunity was missed to establish a framework which allowed for the development of consistency in

---

6   M. Castells, *The Rise of the Network Society* (Oxford: Blackwell, 1996).
7   P. Hennessy, *The Secret State: Whitehall and the Cold War* (London: Penguin, 2003); and 'The British Secret State Old and New' in *RUSI Journal*, Vol. 150, No. 3, pp. 16–22 (London: RUSI, 2005); D. Omand, *The Secret State Revisited* (London: RUSI, 2003; available at www.rusi-journal.com). The terminology has not yet settled between 'protecting state' (Omand) and 'protective state' (Hennessy).

emergency planning across the UK. Second, as events were to show, the Government had no structured processes for detecting and acting on emerging non-terrorist risks which could pose a severe challenge to society. Third, it had no ready mechanism for identifying and understanding the way in which major emergencies could challenge societal interdependencies, generating the disruption of essential services on which the smooth functioning of society is based, with the consequent risks of suffering and, in the worst case, breakdown in social cohesion.

Three major emergencies (the so-called three 'F's) in quick succession at the turn of the millennium exposed those gaps: unusually widespread flooding in 2000; fuel protests in 2000, when the UK ran close to acute shortages of fuel supplies, including those necessary for sustaining essential services; and shortly thereafter the foot-and-mouth epidemic of 2001. All three showed fundamental weaknesses in prior preparedness. More broadly, however, the 'triple whammy' was more effective than a single emergency could have been in exposing weaknesses in governance. Some required the invention on the hoof of crisis co-ordination arrangements at each level of the response, from central government to neighbourhoods. And some exposed inadequate understanding of societal interdependencies, whether, for fuel, the fundamental importance of its ready availability in an era of lean supply chains resting on 'just-in-time' principles or, for foot-and-mouth, the way in which response actions in one area could have greater, unintended consequences in another.

The impact of those events provided the stimulus for a wide range of initiatives involving the centre of government after the 2001 General Election. They signalled recognition that it was no longer adequate to leave responsibility for building preparedness with individual central government departments where, even if it was done, work tended to be stove-piped;

synergies and best practice were not exploited; and, in the absence of challenge, issues were left under the carpet. Thus, machinery-of-government changes led to the creation of a new unit in the Cabinet Office to lead on building resilience across central government and wider afield, and to the establishment of new inter-departmental machinery and Cabinet committees to take work forward; new civil protection legislation was developed; new investment programmes were introduced to enhance preparedness and response capabilities; and substantial increases in funding were provided for those and other programmes.

The threat from international terrorism

A further, substantial stimulus towards fundamental reform was provided by the al-Qaeda attacks in the United States on 11 September 2001, and the resulting new calculus of threat that they ushered in of terrorists with the goal of causing casualties on a massive scale, undeterred by the fear of alienating the public or their own supporters – that is, a scale of terrorist challenge and, importantly, of consequence going well beyond that which the UK had experienced in 30 years of Irish terrorism. Since 2003 the British Government has been implementing a long-term strategy for countering international terrorism and the extremism that lies behind it. During this period the threat has changed in character. The terrorist attacks in London on 7 July 2005 brought home the risk of suicide attacks by British citizens, and the potential scale of the attacks we face and their domestic and international impact were shown by the alleged airline bomb plot in August 2006.

Following those attacks the Government has worked with others to step up and deepen the counter-terrorism effort. Both before and after 7 July additional resources have been provided. The threat posed has both domestic and international elements, with a complex interaction between them. The response, too, needs to be broad-ranging and coherent. This has prompted a public articulation of the strategy[8] and measures to strengthen still further the capacity across government to develop and deliver the plans and programmes necessary to achieve the strategy. The Home Office is the lead department for domestic counter-terrorism. At the same time, an effective counter-terrorism strategy against the type of threat we now face needs to engage the whole of government. The collective support to ministers – and the Prime Minister and the Home Secretary as Chairman of the key committees – has therefore been strengthened as one part of the government response.

The threat from international terrorism, whether in the UK or overseas, is, of course, not new. In the UK's case, our most recent experience was the long-running troubles in Northern Ireland which led to a variety of terrorist attacks.

The Islamist terrorist threat does, however, have a number of important characteristics[9] which make framing and implementing a response particularly difficult:

- It is genuinely international, affecting a wide variety of targets in many countries. Attacks are perpetrated by individuals from the countries concerned and sometimes by outsiders. British citizens involved in terrorist activities have links with terrorist facilitators here and overseas. In this and other respects (e.g. use of the internet) it is an example of 'globalization'.
- The threat comes from a variety of group networks and individuals, in a mix of relationships.
- The terrorists intend to cause mass casualties.

---

8   *Countering International Terrorism: the United Kingdoms Strategy* (London: Stationery Office, CM 6888, 2006).
9   For a somewhat more extended discussion see CM 6888, paras 25–40.

- The people involved are driven by particularly violent and extremist beliefs.

We face considerable uncertainty in sizing the threat in terms of its overseas dimension, the composition and scale of the home-grown threat, and the links between them. The changing nature of known home-grown extremist and terrorist-related activity can be assessed based on intelligence, but our intelligence agencies cannot confidently assess the total scale of the threat, including activity of which they are unaware. Our understanding of the overseas-based threat and links between it and UK citizens is similarly cloudy and depends upon close liaison with overseas governments. It follows that sizing our response is also intrinsically very difficult.

The range and diversity of the threat, and the balance between the external and the home-grown elements in different countries, obviously will impact on how the threat is perceived, described and most effectively countered. Because it has both international and domestic elements, both international and domestic policy need to be brought to bear. For the UK as for other countries, action against the al-Qaeda leadership and the prevention of the creation of further opportunities for terrorist 'safe space' and the development of terrorist infrastructure are of key importance. At the same time, terrorism perpetrated by British citizens is simply a crime and is most appropriately dealt with – wherever possible – by arrest and prosecution. Inevitably our perspective on how best to tackle terrorism has been shaped by our experience of tackling Irish terrorism.

What government seeks to achieve

The aim of government policy, whether in countering international terrorism or responding to a range of other contingencies, is 'to reduce the risk, so that people can go about their daily lives freely and with confidence'. The Government is not promising to eliminate risk: it is seeking to find, with partners and with the public, proportionate responses.

In the counter-terrorist context, the Government's response has been framed in terms of four interlinked goals and policies, laws and programmes to give effect to them:

1. Preventing terrorism by tackling the factors which influence individuals to become extremists and potentially to move on to terrorist action itself.
2. Pursuing terrorists and those who sponsor them.
3. Protecting the public, key national services and British interests overseas.
4. Preparing for the consequences of a terrorist attack.

Two of these four 'P's seek to tackle and reduce the threat, and two to mitigate the consequences of any attack. Frameworks of this broad kind can be seen in a number of countries. In the UK's case the 'Protect' strand benefits from the lessons of dealing with 30 years of Irish terrorism. The 'Prepare' strand is part of a wider reform of our capacity for handling civil contingencies, as I shall go on to discuss. The 'Pursue' strand depends upon effective co-operation between our intelligence agencies and between them and overseas partners. It requires effective co-operation between the Security Service and the police. In both these dimensions the UK has a strong track record in comparison with other countries. It is the 'Prevent' strand which is perhaps the most challenging, in terms of action required domestically and internationally, particularly in the light of the evolution of the domestic terrorist threat from UK citizens.

The 'Prevent' element of the Government's counter-terrorism strategy identifies three principal strands of effort whose breadth illustrates the extent of the challenge:[10]

1. Tackling disadvantage and supporting reform – addressing structural problems in the UK and overseas that may contribute to radicalization, such as inequalities and discrimination.
2. Deterring those who facilitate terrorism and those who encourage others to become terrorists – changing the environment in which seeking to turn others towards extremism and terrorist violence can operate.
3. Engaging in the battle of ideas – challenging the ideologies that extremists believe can justify the use of violence, primarily by helping Muslims who wish to dispute these ideas to do so.

Each strand links to profound and difficult issues about what drives individuals towards extremism, and what drives those so 'radicalized' to become terrorists. The first strand is a huge task with uncertain payback in counter-terrorist terms. In the UK those drawn to terrorism are not themselves particularly disadvantaged, whether in educational or employment terms, although the impact of perceived discrimination affecting them or others in encouraging alienation is difficult to judge. The second strand has raised difficult issues with a variety of Muslim and other communities in framing legislation which protects the human rights of individuals while meeting the clear security threat. And the third involves two-way dialogue – and facilitating such communication by others – both domestically and internationally to uncertain effect.

---

10   See CM 6888, paras 6 and 47–63.

In a number of 'Western' countries, the need to engage more effectively in the 'battle of ideas' has increasingly been recognized. Al-Qaeda's message (the single narrative) has proved effective in indoctrinating potential supporters and motivating violent activity to the extent necessary to sustain a terrorist campaign. The response needs to recognize that the target audience vulnerable to an extremist or terrorism-related message has many different components receiving information through a variety of channels both here and abroad. We need therefore to segment our approach and to ensure that the Government's aims and policies and the realities of life in this country are clearly presented both in the UK and in those overseas countries and media channels which impact on attitudes here. The simplicity of the single narrative needs to be countered by a clear, readily understandable response.

In framing the approach to the 'battle of ideas', both the media and community engagement are of key importance. Al-Qaeda has chosen to frame its essentially political message in religious terms. But this is not in reality an argument about religion, and the response should not be framed in such terms. Similarly community engagement needs to embrace a variety of voices likely to be an influence to different members of our society and, as Amartya Sen has argued,[11] avoid divisions based on a single dominant system of classification, whether in terms of religion, community, civilization, etc. Our interest is in developing and emphasizing the multiple links and loyalties in our society.

Underpinning the four-'P' structure of what we are seeking to achieve, there is recognition of what might in sense be the fifth 'P', that successful delivery depends upon *partnerships* between all parts of government, the public, private and voluntary sectors, and everyone in the UK as individuals and as members of communities.

---

11   A. Sen, *Identity and Violence* (London: Allen Lane, 2006).

Resilience planning

How, then, has planning for major emergencies – including the 'Prepare' element of the Government's counter-terrorism strategy – been developed? Over the past three years, the UK has introduced resilience planning processes based on seven key activities, each of which has to be undertaken effectively if the acid test – of minimizing potential harm from major emergencies – is to be met. These are aggregated into four steps:

1. *Risk identification:* ensuring that organizations at every level, through 'horizon-scanning' and other techniques, routinely identify emerging risks, across the short and medium terms; that they incorporate those risks where appropriate into their risk-assessment processes; and that they share them with others with an interest. Clearly, if a risk is not identified, there is a greater chance that an effective response will not be assembled, or assembled in good time.

2. *Risk assessment:* ensuring that risks are routinely assessed in terms of likelihood and impact, and that those assessments are thorough, balanced and proportionate. The assessments inform the development of a common set of *planning assumptions* for all stakeholders involved in developing response capabilities on the nature and scale of consequences which might need to be addressed – for example, the number of infected people requiring care; the duration and scale of power or telecommunications outages; the number of people requiring rescue from collapsed buildings; or the number of fatalities.

3. *Building resilience*, through drawing down from the planning assumptions via operational analysis and other techniques a set of defined *capability requirements*, specifying the capabilities needed in an ideal world to mount an

effective response to the consequences they portray; agreeing through balance of investment and other forms of prioritization which of those requirements should be funded in departments' core programmes; then putting in place delivery programmes covering the resulting *capability targets*. These are divided into four areas:

- *Generic capabilities:* the generic capabilities (Intensive Treatment Unit beds; personal protective equipment; temporary mortuaries; communications systems) applicable to the response to a range of major emergencies.
- *Specific capabilities:* individual capabilities (e.g. H5N1 vaccine) required to permit an effective response to individual risks, in areas where it would not be prudent to rely on the mobilization of generic capabilities alone.
- *Crisis management capability:* ensuring that those organizations with a key leadership role in a major emergency have the staff, aptitudes, skills and experience to discharge that role effectively.
- *Business continuity management arrangements:* ensuring that organizations at every level in the UK and in every sector who have a role in the response to or recovery from a major emergency, or whose actions will be important in absorbing and minimizing its indirect impact, have in place effective business continuity plans so that they are not prevented by the emergency from mobilizing their response.

4. *Evaluation:* providing assurance of the adequacy of plans and capabilities, and hence of the UK's preparedness to respond to major emergencies, through an honest performance-management regime (including a national self-evaluation survey) and processes to learn the lessons of major operations and exercises.

The activities described above are essentially iterative. But they cannot be for central government alone. Thus a key goal in the operation of these processes, supported in some areas by the duties set out in the Civil Contingencies Act, is to secure consistency in preparedness planning through harmonizing processes and underpinning analysis where relevant across all levels in the UK. As a result, in relevant areas information and guidance are passed up and down the chain from central government to local responders. And, where appropriate (e.g. in risk assessment), central government sets out the framework and practices to be adopted at all levels.

Building involvement

Everyone, then, has a role to play in building preparedness. State practitioners have responsibilities for ensuring public safety. Businesses can help to minimize impact through sustaining essential services. Individual citizens can contribute through their involvement in voluntary groups. They can, too, help themselves and those around them. The potential scope of civil protection in twenty-first-century society is well recognized in civil protection planning in France, promoted as being '*laffaire du tous*', and in other European states (e.g. the Nordic countries) with historically devolved governance structures coupled with relatively higher degrees of citizen participation. The need to harness a genuinely national effort has historically been less well recognized in the UK. As the Lessons to be Learned Inquiry on the 2001 foot-and-mouth epidemic noted:

> Whatever central government does and however well, it cannot defeat a major outbreak of animal disease on its own. It needs to co-ordinate the support and services of many others, including those most directly affected . . . Wholehearted support for a common purpose depends

on mutual trust and confidence . . . [these] cannot be built by the independent actions of one side alone.[12]

Thus, a key challenge for civil protection planning in the UK is to enable the active involvement of all sections of society. The ideal governance framework would encompass the actions of government at central, regional and local levels; of corporate hierarchies, especially in their business continuity planning; of associations, especially practitioner societies, organizations in the voluntary sector, and faith groups; of communities and networks; and of individual citizens.

A governance framework which mobilizes this broad range of actors is clearly challenging to operate. It requires clarity of purpose, although it is thankfully easy to define this – as far as possible ensuring people's safety and well-being – and to describe its components – reducing the potential impact of major emergencies on citizens' health, social welfare and economic prosperity. It needs effective communication of the case for and benefits from engagement. And it needs a readily understood legal framework that finds the right balance between central prescription (to ensure the necessary consistency of action across the UK and the continued observance of national standards), and permissiveness (to allow local solutions to be found to local challenges).

Parliament has passed legislation – the Civil Contingencies Act 2004 – which seeks to establish a clear set of roles and responsibilities for local responders; greater structure and consistency in civil protection activity; better communication among local responders; and a sound basis for effective performance management. It includes both functional and collaborative duties to achieve these goals, requiring those

---

12 I. Anderson *et al.*, *Foot and Mouth Disease 2001: Lessons to be Learned Inquiry Report* (London: Stationery Office, HC 888, 2002).

'Category 1' responders at the core of emergency response (e.g. the police, emergency services, local authorities, health bodies) to undertake:

1. *Risk assessment:* to assess the risk of emergencies occurring and use this to inform contingency planning.
2. *Emergency planning:* to put in place emergency plans, exercise them to ensure that they are effective, and offer training to staff who may become involved in emergency response.
3. *Business continuity management:* to put in place business continuity plans to ensure that responder organizations can continue to exercise critical functions in the event of an emergency.
4. *Public communications:* to put in place arrangements to make information available to the public about civil protection matters in advance of an emergency; and maintain arrangements to warn, inform and advise the public in the event of an emergency.
5. *Information sharing:* to share information with other local responders, to enhance co-ordination, on the rationalist assumption that maximizing its availability to those who need it in building preparedness will maximize the quality of decision-making.
6. *Co-operation:* to co-operate with other local responders to enhance co-ordination and efficiency.
7. *Business continuity management promotion:* to provide advice and assistance to businesses and voluntary organizations about business continuity management (local authorities only).

The Act also defines a group of co-operating bodies ('Category 2' responders) who are less likely to be at the heart of planning work but will be heavily involved in incidents that affect their sector (e.g. utilities). Under the Act, these bodies are required to co-operate and share information with other Category 1 and 2 responders to ensure that they are well integrated within wider emergency-planning frameworks.

The governance framework put in place needs to include co-operative processes which guide the work of those involved so that it is undertaken on a consistent basis, as well as processes which enforce consistency where necessary. The UK Government has used legislation for both purposes, both in enabling co-operation and action through the permissive powers it provides and in forcing action through the duties it imposes, underpinned by performance-audit regimes for the major public bodies concerned. And, in contrast to the limited amount of best-practice guidance published by the Government in the late 1990s, that which underpins the new Act[13] runs to over 300 pages.

As a further motivating force, in parallel with the passage of the new legislation described above, the UK Government also more than doubled the amount of money it made available in grant to local authorities, to allow them to undertake the duties set out in the legislation (indeed, the grant was increased to a level slightly above local authorities' own estimate of the sums they needed).

In considering how best to ensure the involvement of businesses, policy-making has had to consider how far market forces will drive desired behaviour: will firms themselves see business benefit, rather than business burden, from engaging in relevant planning? In the UK, this has led to the need to consider carefully the right balance between, on the one hand,

---

13 *Emergency Preparedness: Guidance on Part 1 of the Civil Contingencies Act 2004, its associated Regulations and Non-statutory Arrangements* (York: Emergency Planning College, 2005); and *Emergency Response and Recovery: Non-statutory Guidance to Complement Emergency Preparedness* (York: Emergency Planning College, 2005).

placing preparedness duties in law on the business sector that mirror those placed on public-sector bodies; and, on the other, a strong desire to reduce the burden of regulation on business, a high current priority for the Government. In the end, the Government decided that it would not seek through the Civil Contingencies Act to place statutory business-continuity duties on businesses, even those within the Critical National Infrastructure, but would encourage their voluntary engagement in preparedness work, through the mechanisms described above.

The challenge of gaining the involvement of the wider community has been only partially met, so far. A first step was to reverse the legacy of Cold War secretiveness, and to establish a governance framework which gave observable permission to the involvement not only of governmental practitioners but also of non-practitioners in associations and communities, down to the level of individual citizens. There have been four further steps towards implementation of this aim:

1. The establishment of Regional Resilience Forums in each region of England and Wales, and beneath them Local Resilience Forums at broadly county level, bringing together not only governmental practitioners but also businesses, and voluntary and community groups.

2. The progressive implementation of the duties under the Civil Contingencies Act of local policy development and communication with the public has driven the greater, and earlier, integration of both. That has in turn provided the conditions for practitioners and non-practitioners to discuss individual issues at a considerable level of detail, in a way which is meaningful to their particular circumstances, facilitated by the duty in the Act on participants to share information. (It has also prompted those involved in policy development to think through much earlier how best to communicate their messages to practitioners and the public.)

3. The creation at both national and regional levels of mechanisms to engage the business community in either generic resilience activity (with a particular focus on sharing information about risks, and on business continuity planning against those risks) or work focused on building preparedness for specific major risks (e.g. an influenza pandemic).

4. The establishment of a concordat between local government, the emergency services and the voluntary sector covering their involvement in building resilience, underpinned by a duty in legislation on government practitioners to have due regard in their planning for the capabilities of voluntary agencies. This spirit of partnership is given practical expression through a number of committees on either generic or specific preparedness issues.

Less progress has been made in the engagement of individual citizens, or of neighbourhoods. In 2004, the Government issued a booklet[14] to all households in the UK, providing basic information on its perception of the risks facing the UK and describing some simple, practical steps which citizens could take to build their own preparedness for a range of emergencies, from domestic accidents upwards. However, there remains strong but under-developed potential to build 'community resilience' through the preparations made in neighbourhoods and social groups for individuals to provide practical support to their less advantaged neighbours in the event of major emergencies.

Relationships and trust

Pivotal to the effective operation of the governance framework, the processes described above and efforts to ensure

---

14   *Preparing for Emergencies* (www.pfe.gov.uk).

consistency, is clarity of understanding by all participants of their and others' respective roles, including the ability of some to set standards and boundaries. Thus, for example, one key test in taking work forward is whether non-practitioners, especially citizens and community groups, who choose to become engaged in preparedness planning can readily differentiate who is responsible for what. A second is whether leaders, formal and informal, are clear about their roles, and about the boundaries around their work.

The work of the past three years has also exposed interesting issues of trust. A basic level of trust between parties is clearly essential in any field of activity to sustain and deepen collaboration over time. But trust is a particularly acute issue in counter-terrorism and civil protection.

In the case of counter-terrorism, success in part depends on reducing the pool of those who might be radicalized and, among the radicalized, those who might in turn cross over to become terrorists. This requires community cohesion and shared values and goals. Steps taken in one element of the counter-terrorism agenda – for example, the pursuit of terrorist suspects – can risk cutting across the 'Prevent' element.

In the context of civil protection, the collaborative arrangements used and the personal relationships built in preparedness planning will be drawn on heavily in the response to a major emergency. And associated with trust are respect and credibility. Civil protection is a field populated by professions which continue to command both.[15] (Equally, as was demonstrated in the aftermath of the response to Hurricane Katrina in events leading to the resignation of the Director of the US Federal Emergency Management Agency, the opposite can be

---

15   M. Granatt, 'On Trust: Using Public Information and Warning Partnerships to Support the Community Response in an Emergency' in *Journal of Communication Management*, Vol. 8, No. 4 (2004), pp. 354–65.

savagely true.) Those professionals will inevitably have a significant influence in the day-to-day operation of governance structures. Perhaps as a result, the chairmen of most of the Local Resilience Forums described above tend to be senior police officers, despite the police having no formal leadership role in the response to the most challenging wide-area emergencies, such as an influenza pandemic.[16]

Communications

The analysis above has drawn out the importance of communications with those who need to have a designated role, at different levels. There is also a high need for communications with those who are not so engaged (the 'general public'). This involves reputation management for the usual reasons, but goes well beyond it to preparing the public to receive and act on messages from the Government and practitioners which will enable them to secure their own safety in an emergency.

The resulting communications strategy adopted in the UK has four key elements:

1. To *inform* and *desensitize*, seeking to strip away unnecessary secrecy, debunk conspiracy theories and prevent the existence of a void for others to fill.
2. To *demonstrate* competence and coherence (plans and actions together).
3. To *reassure* and build confidence and trust.
4. To help *build public resilience* by instilling life-conditioning behaviour, before and after a crisis.

---

16 Some 65 per cent of Local Resilience Forums are currently chaired by senior police officers, some 25 per cent by local authority officers, and the rest by people from other bodies, chosen by colleagues because of their enthusiasm and aptitude.

A key enabler to this is the provision of information which is as full, honest and candid as possible, allowing people to draw their own conclusions about the competence of response arrangements, hence allowing them to build confidence and trust. The desirable, if idealized, first end goal can be summed up as the public perceiving that 'we are prepared for emergencies, and I know my interests are being looked after'. Atomized against the analysis above, this becomes 'There is a strategy; it is well thought through and coherent; it is being implemented by organizations working together; someone visible and accountable is in charge; and it is delivering real improvements.' The second, again idealized, end goal is the reciprocal of this – a public which is alert, attentive and prepared, and willing to say 'I am prepared. I know what I should do to take care of myself and others.'

Research suggests that the public can be split into two groups, for each of whom a different approach is needed to achieve these end goals. A high proportion of the general public would be happy with a general feeling of reassurance and positively does not want to be asked to think in any depth about emergencies and the response to them. For this group, there is a high risk of backlash if they perceive that too much information is being thrust on them. Those in this group want to be left to get on with their lives, not to live in fear. Conversely, a smaller group actively seeks answers to factual questions and visible evidence of action and improvement before they are ready to feel reassured. Within this group, there are specific communities who want bespoke information to help them to carry out their responsibilities – business and domestic. These communities include businesses, schools and parents. There is some evidence that suggests that women may be more concerned, active and demanding than men.

Research also suggests that the public is most appreciative of messages about *what* to expect and *how* to respond. As in other public-policy fields, most interest is focused on issues that have a local resonance. In the civil protection field, that means local responses to local incidents, so that material from local councils which refers to local hazards and to familiar resources and channels of communications seems the most influential. Again, as in many other fields, research also offers a clear pointer on *who* should transmit the messages – respected and trusted practitioners, who have greater credibility than politicians or policy-makers.

The UK resilience communications strategy reflects this research. It thus covers not only messages transmitted by ministers and policy-makers directly to the public but also those from respected practitioners. And it has national and local dimensions. It is possible to detect a growing level of information being made available at the local level, although it remains patchy in content (with a greater focus on risk than response) and coverage (some councils are markedly better than others). In parallel, the creation and development of Regional Media Emergency Forums (comprising media organizations, local authorities, the emergency services, government agencies and the utilities) and the corresponding communications groups of Local Resilience Forums have led to the development of closer working relationships between all stakeholders in co-ordinating, developing and ultimately delivering information to the media and thence to the public.

Communications activity at national level covers preparedness planning which is a matter of national concern (e.g. influenza pandemic preparedness), which is demonstrably led from the centre of government. It also covers work undertaken by national organizations as part of a nationwide campaign, albeit with local application, associated with the discharge of their responsibilities (e.g. preparedness for coastal and fluvial flooding, led by the UK's Environment Agency). And it covers

areas (e.g. business continuity planning) where it is most efficient for the campaign to be led centrally, involving stakeholders from representative organizations able to cascade material
to their members, albeit with reinforcement from regional and
local groups.

It is too early to draw conclusions on whether this work is
generating success in meeting the end goals described above.
It is possible to be reasonably confident about a first acid test
– that the level of public debate about the risk of major
emergencies arising is roughly proportionate to current
official assessments of the likelihood of those risks and of
their consequences. As a result, there is less chance of 'cold
calling' – of events which the public is likely to consider to be
forecastable coming as a shock, with all of the damage that
that can do to the Government's reputation and hence public
confidence in the Government's ability to manage the
response.

It is also beginning to be possible to draw communications
lessons from the response to recent emergencies. For example,
the public-information element of the communications
strategy response to the bombings in London in July 2005 was
judged to be generally successful. One of the key factors in this
success was the close working relationship developed between
government communicators and colleagues in the police and
emergency services, local authorities and transport operators.
That co-operation meant that all involved recognized the
importance of ensuring that the Government delivered its key
messages without being seen to step over the invisible dividing
line into the area of operational communications. At the same
time, a number of weaknesses have been identified and tackled
about the information available through the Casualty Bureau,
the Family Assistance Centre and other areas of concern to
bereaved families and survivors. Striking the right balance
between recognizing the clear concerns of the bereaved and

injured while recognizing the heroism on the day of all those who responded to the emergency has proved to be one of the most difficult communications issues.[17]

Conclusion

Since the low point of the three 'F's at the turn of the century, considerable effort has been put into new organizational approaches at every level of government – better processes, more investment in new capability, and so on. Approaches to counter-terrorism and to civil preparedness have been fundamentally revamped to reflect the post-Cold War, al-Qaeda world in which we live. The scale of the change, including at the centre of government, may not be sufficiently understood. The extent of the orchestration required involving partnerships of various kinds across our society is clear. Equally we need to recognize the scale and breadth of the challenge in seeking to secure the safety and welfare of citizens against the shocks that have the potential to disrupt the complex, interdependent society of the twenty-first century.

In tackling these challenges, citizens have an important part to play in securing their own and their neighbour's safety. They will, however, place their actions within a framework of two expectations of the Government – that it will manage effectively its part of the response; and that it will be honest in providing the information needed to allow people to take the steps necessary to maximize their own safety.

---

17 *Addressing Lessons from the Emergency Response to the 7 July 2005 London Bombings* (HM Government, 2006).

3

The International Terrorist Threat to the United Kingdom

Eliza Manningham-Buller

I have been Director General of the Security Service (MI5) since 2002. Before that I was Deputy Director General for five years. During that time, and before, I have witnessed a steady increase in the terrorist threat to the UK. It has been the subject of much comment and controversy. I rarely speak in public. I prefer to avoid the limelight and get on with my job. But today,* I want to set out my views on the realities of the terrorist threat facing the UK in 2006, what motivates those who pose that threat and what my Service is doing, with others, to counter it. I speak not as a politician, nor as a pundit, but as someone who has been an intelligence professional for 32 years.

Five years on from 9/11, where are we? Speaking in August 2006, Deputy Assistant Commissioner Peter Clarke, the head of the Anti-Terrorist Branch of the Metropolitan Police, described the threat to the UK from al-Qaeda-related terrorism as 'real, here, deadly and enduring'. Only recently the Home Secretary said the threat will be 'enduring – the struggle will be long and wide and deep'. Let me describe more fully why I think they said that.

---

*9 November 2006 at the Mile End Institute, Queen Mary, University of London.

We now know that the first al-Qaeda-related plot against the UK was the one we discovered and disrupted in November 2000 in Birmingham. A British citizen is currently serving a long prison sentence for plotting to detonate a large bomb in the UK. Let there be no doubt about this: the international terrorist threat to this country is not new. It began before Iraq, before Afghanistan, and before 9/11.

In the years after 9/11, with atrocities taking place in Madrid, Casablanca, Bali, Istanbul and elsewhere, terrorists plotted to mount a string of attacks in the UK, but were disrupted. This run of domestic success was interrupted tragically in London in July 2005. Since then, the combined efforts of my Service, the police, Secret Intelligence Service (SIS) and Government Communications Headquarters (GCHQ) have thwarted a further five major conspiracies in the UK, saving many hundreds (possibly even thousands) of lives.

Recently the Lord Chancellor said that there were a total of 99 defendants awaiting trial in 34 cases. Of course the presumption of innocence applies and the law dictates that nothing must be said or done which might prejudice the right of a defendant to receive a fair trial. You will understand therefore that I can say no more on these matters.

What I can say is that today, my officers and the police are working to contend with some 200 groupings or networks, totalling over 1,600 identified individuals (and there will be many we don't know of) who are actively engaged in plotting, or facilitating, terrorist acts here and overseas. The extremists are motivated by a sense of grievance and injustice driven by their interpretation of the history between the West and the Muslim world. This view is shared, in some degree, by a far wider constituency. If the opinion polls conducted in the UK since July 2005 are only broadly accurate, over 100,000 of our citizens consider that the July 2005 attacks in London were justified.

What we see at the extreme end of the spectrum are resilient networks, some directed from al-Qaeda in Pakistan, some more loosely inspired by it, planning attacks including mass-casualty suicide attacks in the UK. Today we see the use of home-made improvised explosive devices; tomorrow's threat may include the use of chemicals, bacteriological agents, radioactive materials and even nuclear technology. More and more people are moving from passive sympathy towards active terrorism through being radicalized or indoctrinated by friends, families, in organized training events here and overseas, by images on television, through chat rooms and websites on the internet.

The propaganda machine is sophisticated and al-Qaeda itself says that 50 per cent of its war is conducted through the media. In Iraq, attacks are regularly videoed and the footage downloaded onto the internet within 30 minutes. Virtual media teams then edit the result, translate it into English and many other languages, and package it for a worldwide audience. And, chillingly, we see the results here – young teenagers being groomed to be suicide bombers.

We are aware of numerous plots to kill people and to damage our economy. What do I mean by numerous? Five? Ten? No, nearer 30, that we know of. These plots often have links back to al-Qaeda in Pakistan and through those links al-Qaeda gives guidance and training to its largely British foot soldiers here on an extensive and growing scale. And it is not just the UK of course. Other countries also face a new terrorist threat, from Spain to France to Canada and Germany.

A word on proportionality. My Service and the police have occasionally been accused of hype and lack of perspective – or worse, of deliberately stirring up fear. It is difficult to argue that there are not worse problems facing us – for example, climate change . . . and of course far more people are killed each year on the roads than die through terrorism. It is understandable that people are reluctant to accept assertions that do not always appear to be substantiated. It is right to be sceptical about intelligence. I shall say more about that later.

But just consider this. A terrorist spectacular would cost potentially thousands of lives and do major damage to the world economy. Imagine if a plot to bring down several passenger aircraft succeeded – thousands dead, major economic damage, disruption across the globe. And al-Qaeda is an organization without restraint.

There has been much speculation about what motivates young men and women to carry out acts of terrorism in the UK. My Service needs to understand the motivations behind terrorism in order to succeed in countering it, as far as that is possible. Al-Qaeda has developed an ideology which claims that Islam is under attack, and needs to be defended.

This is a powerful narrative that weaves together conflicts from across the globe, presenting the West's response to varied and complex issues, from long-standing disputes such as Israel/Palestine and Kashmir to more recent events as evidence of an across-the-board determination to undermine and humiliate Islam worldwide. Afghanistan, the Balkans, Chechnya, Iraq, Israel/Palestine, Kashmir and Lebanon are regularly cited by those who advocate terrorist violence as illustrating what they allege is Western hostility to Islam.

The video wills of British suicide bombers make it clear that they are motivated by perceived worldwide and long-standing injustices against Muslims, an extreme and minority interpretation of Islam promoted by some preachers and people of influence, and their interpretation as anti-Muslim of UK foreign policy, in particular the UK's involvement in Iraq and Afghanistan.

Killing oneself and others in response is an attractive option for some citizens of this country and others around the world.

What intelligence can do

As I said earlier, I have been an intelligence officer for some 32 years. And I want again to describe what intelligence is and is not. I wish life were like *Spooks*, where everything is knowable, and soluble by six people. But those whose plans we wish to detect in advance are determined to conceal from us what they intend to do. And every day they learn – from the mistakes of others, from what they discover of our capabilities from evidence presented in court and from leaks to the media.

Moreover, intelligence is usually bitty and needs piecing together, assessing, judging. It takes objectivity, integrity and a sceptical eye to make good use of intelligence: even the best of it never tells the whole story. On the basis of such incomplete information, my Service and the police make decisions on when and how to take action, to protect public safety. Wherever possible we seek to collect evidence sufficient to secure prosecutions, but it is not always possible to do so: admissible evidence is not always available, and the courts, rightly, look for a high standard of certainty. Often to protect public safety the police need to disrupt plots on the basis of intelligence but before evidence sufficient to bring criminal charges has been collected.

We are faced by acute and very difficult choices of prioritization. We cannot focus on everything so we have to decide on a daily basis with the police and others where to focus our energies, whom to follow, whose telephone lines need listening to, which seized media needs to go to the top of the analytic pile. Because of the sheer scale of what we face, the task is daunting. We won't always make the right choices. And we recognize that we shall have scarce sympathy if we are unable to prevent one of our targets committing an atrocity.

And the Service?

As I speak, my staff, roughly 2,800 of them (an increase of almost 50 per cent since 9/11, 25 per cent under 30, over 6 per cent from ethnic minorities, with 52 languages, with links to well over 100 services worldwide), are working very hard, at some cost to their private lives and in some cases their safety, to do their utmost to collect the intelligence we need.

The first challenge is to find those who would cause us harm, among the 60 million or so people who live here and the hundreds of thousands who visit each year. That is no easy task, particularly given the scale and speed of radicalization and the age of some being radicalized.

The next stage is to decide what action to take in response to that intelligence. Who are merely talking big, and who have real ambitions? Who have genuine aspirations to commit terrorism, but lack the know-how or materials? Who are the skilled and trained ones, who the amateurs? Where should we and the police focus our finite resources? It's a hard grind but my staff are highly motivated, conscious of the risks they carry individually, and aware that they may not be able to do enough to stop the next attack. We owe them a tremendous debt of gratitude and I thank them.

On 8 July 2005 I spoke to all my staff. I said that what we feared would happen had finally happened. I reminded them that we had warned that it was a matter of when, not if, and that they were trained to respond – indeed, many had been up all night, from the intelligence staff to the catering staff. I told them that we had received many messages of support from around the world, and that we, along with our colleagues in the police and emergency services, were in the privileged position of being able to make a difference. And we did. And we have done so since.

My Service is growing very rapidly. By 2008 it will be twice the size it was at 9/11. We know much more than we did then. We have developed new techniques, new sources, new relationships. We understand much better the scale and nature of what we are tackling, but much is still obscure and radicalization continues. Moreover, even with such rapid growth, we shall not be able to investigate nearly enough of the problem, so the prioritization I mentioned earlier will remain essential but risky. And new intelligence officers need to be trained. That takes time, as does the acquisition of experience, the experience that helps one with those difficult choices and tough judgements.

What else can others do?

That brings me on to my final point. None of this can be tackled by my Service alone. Others have to address the causes, counter the radicalization, assist in the rehabilitation of those affected, and work to protect our way of life. We have key partners, the police being the main ones, and I'd like to applaud those police officers working alongside us on this huge challenge, those who collect intelligence beside us, help convert it into evidence for court, and face the dangers of arresting individuals who have no concern for their own lives or the lives of others. The scale and seriousness of the threat means that others play vital roles – SIS and GCHQ collecting key intelligence overseas, other services internationally who recognize the global nature of the problem, government departments, business and the public.

Safety for us all means working together to protect those we care about, being alert to the danger without over-reacting, and reporting concerns. We need to be alert to attempts to radicalize and indoctrinate our youth and to seek to counter it. Radicalizing elements within communities are trying to exploit grievances for terrorist purposes. It is the youth who are being actively targeted, groomed, radicalized and set on a path that frighteningly quickly could end in their involvement in mass murder of their fellow UK citizens, or their early death in a suicide attack or on a foreign battlefield.

We also need to understand some of the differences between non-Western and Western lifestyles and not treat people with suspicion because of their religion, or, indeed, to confuse fundamentalism with terrorism. We must realize that there are significant differences between faiths and communities within our society, and most people, from whatever origin, condemn all acts of terror in the UK. And we must focus on those values that we all share in this country regardless of our background: equality, freedom, justice and tolerance. Many people are working for and with us to address the threat precisely for those reasons, because all of us, whatever our ethnicity and faith, are the targets of the terrorists.

I have spoken as an intelligence professional, describing the reality of terrorism and counter-terrorism in the UK at the present time. My messages are sober ones. I do not speak in this way to alarm (nor, as the cynics might claim, to enhance the reputation of my organization) but to give the most frank account I can of the al-Qaeda threat to the UK. That threat is serious, is growing and will, I believe, be with us for a generation. It is a sustained campaign, not a series of isolated incidents. It aims to wear down our will to resist.

My Service is dedicated to tackling the deadly manifestations of terrorism. Tackling its roots is the work of us all.

4

Countering International Terrorism: Joining Up the Dots

Kevin Tebbit

It is a great honour for me to deliver this, my first lecture as a Visiting Professor in the Department of History at Queen Mary, University of London. And it is a particular pleasure to do so as a presentation to the Mile End Group, with whom I already enjoy a close association.

The subject I have chosen is topical, and the territory is well trodden. Much has been published recently, by the Government and by informed 'insiders' about the nature of the threat from international terrorism and the strategies to counter it. In July, the Government published a Command paper, setting out the latest iteration of its strategy, designed to ensure that 'people can go about their daily lives freely and with confidence'.[1] This was amplified by the senior responsible official, Sir Richard Mottram, in a lecture given here at Queen Mary.[2] The important intelligence dimension has also been discussed extensively over the past year, stimulated not least by Sir David Omand, another authoritative figure and a founding father of the strategy itself.[3]

---

1   *Countering International Terrorism: The United Kingdom's Strategy*, CM6888 (London: Stationery Office, July 2006).
2   R. Mottram, *Protecting the Citizen in the 21st Century: Issues and Challenges* (London: Queen Mary College, 2006) [i.e. Chapter 2 of this book].
3   D. Omand, *Reflections on Secret Intelligence* (London: Gresham College, 2005) [i.e. Chapter 5 of this book].

Now, it is not my purpose to go over all the same ground that has already been covered thoroughly. What I want to do is to offer some perspectives on a different part of the subject – the role of defence concepts and military force, in both domestic and foreign policy contexts; not because it is the most controversial aspect – though that is certainly the case; nor simply as a result of my own recent experiences professionally; but because this dimension has been virtually absent from much of the recent government and academic discourse. Why the military dimension is missing and how far it should be reinstated is the main theme of my address.

My starting point is to outline what I take to be common ground, for both government and mainstream commentators, about the nature of the threat from terrorism and the strategy to counter it.

On the threat itself there is broad agreement about its key features. These are as follows.

1. That it is not a passing phase, or the work of a tiny criminal fringe, to which governments have overreacted, but a phenomenon that is here to stay, requiring a similarly long-term response from us.
2. That it is international in scope – in a sense facilitated by globalization – and, self-evidently, therefore, not something any one country can deal with by a national strategy alone.
3. That it is potentially strategic in effect, not least because of the terrorists' apparent determination to create maximum damage, including the ambition to acquire weapons of mass destruction.
4. That it is simple at one level in its objectives: the overturn of Western influence and values in various parts of the world and their replacement by strict Islamic regimes or fundamentalist theocracies. But complex in its operation,

given the variety of different individuals and groups involved – in Iraq, Afghanistan, Pakistan, Europe and elsewhere in the Middle East, Africa and Asia – and the loose nature of their networks, not least in relation to al-Qaeda itself, which is now more an inspiration for attacks on Western interests than a central organization of direct control.

The UK Government's strategy seeks to deal comprehensively with the threat, and is organized around four themes: Prevent, Pursue, Protect and Prepare. 'Prevent' aims to address root causes: of poor governance, political alienation, economic and social inequalities, while at the same time seeking to deter by various means those who would sponsor or facilitate terrorist action. 'Pursue' recognizes the need for this to be accompanied in current circumstances by coercive, disruptive or destructive action by security forces, at home and overseas, informed by good intelligence. 'Protect' involves the security of the public, our borders, critical national infrastructure and British interests overseas. 'Prepare' emphasizes the importance of building the understanding and capacity to deal with the consequences of a terrorist attack, should it occur, mainly on the lines of improved civil emergency planning and broad public awareness.

The Government has programmes in place for each of the four 'P's (stronger in some areas than others) and has underlined the importance it attaches to them and its plans to do more. Sir Richard Mottram has vividly contrasted the difference between security management during the Cold War, which was essentially the exclusive business of the state and its agents, most obviously the Armed Forces, and the post-9/11 world where a much broader combination of relationships must come into play – state, private sector and communities working together in order to build the necessary protection and resilience.

Sir David Omand[4] has highlighted the vital importance of knowledge and intelligence, so that security countermeasures can be applied selectively, with precision, and preferably before an attack takes place, as in the recent (August 2006) Operation Overt. Good intelligence is clearly vital in easing the dilemma of needing to act to save life without causing excessive disruption to people's daily lives; or, indeed, without alienating the very communities and countries whose co-operation and active help are needed in order to root out and isolate jihadist terrorism from Muslim society.

So much, as I say, I take to be common ground. Now to the role of military force.

The Armed Forces do, of course, have a long and distinguished history, both in combating terrorism itself in the UK and overseas and in helping with civil emergencies from whatever cause. Military doctrine and techniques have been built up from operational experience in Malaya, Oman, Northern Ireland, the Balkans, Sierra Leone, and Afghanistan. They are being applied today in Iraq and Afghanistan. As regards military aid to our civil community, few who experienced the succession of emergencies of 2000 and 2001 will forget the role played by Armed Forces in helping to cope with the consequences of the four 'F's: the widespread flooding; the fuel protests – which threatened essential services and the life of the country; the foot-and-mouth epidemic, which, if anything, had a greater impact at the time; and the Services' role in providing emergency cover during industrial action by the firemen more recently. At the same time as preparing for the Iraq operation in 2003, the MOD were still training 19,000 servicemen and women as contingency firefighters.

---

4   See Chapter 7.

Yet despite this background, there is hardly a mention of the military dimension in any of the recent government policy statements. It is almost as if the new security challenges that confront society are seen as being so very different from the past that they call for a response in which the role of Armed Forces is marginal at best. Whereas before, defence strategy and military force was central to the preservation of Western security, there is only a brief reference to them in the strategy of the four 'P's. A reader of the July 2006 White Paper will have to get to paragraph 87 before finding a mention, and then only cursorily. And in his lecture about the UK counter-terrorist strategy delivered here, Sir Richard Mottram did not refer to the role of military force at all.

Now, I am not about to suggest that the threats we face today are akin to the security challenges of the past or call for Armed Forces to be used in the same way as before. The shift from what Peter Hennessy has described as the Secret State of the Cold War to the Protective State of today has been well documented by him and others.[5] There are three principal changes that affect the military role.

First, as I myself have argued in an earlier lecture else-where,[6] the Cold War was actually non-violent, really a confrontation in which force was deliberately withheld by both sides, and deterrence worked successfully; whereas now deterrence is not working in this area: violence is being employed as an active and deadly instrument against us for real.

Second, in the past we could rely on a security posture that was almost entirely external, on the North German Plain, or beneath the Atlantic; and such enforcement action that was needed to protect our interests, whether in the Falklands or

---

5   P. Hennessy, *The Secret State and the Cold War* (London: Penguin, 2003); 'The Secret State: Old and New' (London: *RUSI Journal*, Vol. 150, No. 3, 2005); and D. Omand, *The Secret State Revisited* (RUSI, 2003).
6   K. Tebbit, Peter Nailor Memorial Lecture, Gresham College, London, 2003.

subsequent to the Cold War, could be undertaken exclusively abroad by the Armed Forces. Now, after the bombings of July 2005 and Operation Overt, to disrupt the alleged aircraft bomb plot, the most immediate threat is seen to be internal, from the phenomenon of 'home-grown' terrorists, British citizens who use a distorted version of the Islamic faith to justify violence in the UK. And the security lead in countering this has naturally moved to the domestic civil authorities.

Third, we are no longer dealing with conflict between states. General Sir Rupert Smith, in his book on the utility of force,[7] argues that there has been a paradigm shift from what he terms 'interstate industrial war' to 'war amongst the people'. 'Our opponents', he says, 'are formless and their leaders and operatives are outside the structures in which we order the world and society. The threats they pose are not directly to our states or territories, but to the security of our people, of other peoples, our assets and way of life so as to change our intentions and have their way.'[8]

Clearly in these changed circumstances, the role to be played by Armed Forces is different from before. It is also understandable that questions have been raised about the utility of military force in counter-terrorism, particularly when terrorists do not rely on state sponsorship or support, as is mainly – but not exclusively – the case today, and offer fleeting targets at best. There are significant complications about the feasibility of achieving successful action, in a direct military sense. There are surrounding legal complications – effectively illustrated, incidentally, for those who watched it, by the TV dramatization *The Path to 9/11*. And crucially, there is the challenge for our governments of ensuring that such action takes place within a wider policy framework, in which military

---

7   R. Smith, *The Utility of Force: The Art of War in the Modern World* (London: Penguin, 2006).

8   *Ibid.*, p. 372.

force is not used separately, still less as an end in itself, but operates as an integral element in comprehensive plans to achieve a desired result (which is political rather than military) and advances those policy objectives – restoring stability, ending repression, fostering democracy and prosperity, or whatever the aim might be.

There is also no denying that mistakes have been made in appreciating the changes and adjusting to them in the way military force is used. Richard Clarke, the former US National Security Council terrorism co-ordinator, has argued, for example,[9] that a main reason for what he sees as the failure of US counter-terrorism strategy was the White House conviction that 'behind every terrorist network there is a state that protects and sponsors it (so that) once such a state is destroyed, the terrorist network and the threat it posed will come to an end'. Clearly neither al-Qaeda nor Iraq fitted within that analytical framework. And the relentless stream of bad news from Iraq and now Afghanistan does not help anyone seeking to make the case for the beneficial application of military force.

Nevertheless, despite the problems, I believe it is worth looking more closely at the way the UK's own defence concepts have evolved since the end of the Cold War, and at the Armed Forces' continuing role and contribution. In my view there is more that is relevant to countering terrorism and to dealing effectively with the security challenges of the twenty-first century than is to be found in the published strategy that I mentioned at the beginning. The need, I suggest, is not to doubt or downgrade the value of military force, but to apply lessons learned from past experience – and to do so on an international and coalition basis, so that it can be harnessed more effectively to agreed purposes in future.

---

9   R. Clarke, *Against All Enemies: Inside America's War on Terror* (New York: Free Press, 2004).

Furthermore, despite the paradigm shift in the security environment in one sense, there are characteristics of the defence posture which served Western democracies well in the Cold War – not least political solidarity and military burden-sharing of risks and responsibilities – which may well need to be rediscovered if we are to deal successfully with radical Islam and its terrorist dimension in future.

So let me examine this military role further, beginning with the UK defence contribution to counter terrorism so far.

In the aftermath of 9/11 the MOD conducted a full review of the UK's defence posture and plans. They held public consultations over the winter and spring of 2002 and published the results in what was called the New Chapter to the Defence Review, in July of that year.[10]

The New Chapter was the first major Government statement of counter-terrorist policy after 9/11. Why should this have come from the Ministry of Defence, rather than the Foreign Office, Cabinet Office or Home Office? There were those in Whitehall at the time who claimed that the MOD was engaged in little more than a presentational manoeuvre, a pre-emptive strike, designed to protect its existing defence programme – what one of them called 'keeping the same old show on the road' – and prevent resources being diverted away from overseas roles and into home defence. But to those of us involved in the process at the time it was more a sense of needing to deal actively with the real issues as they were then arising. Remember, this was the period when the focus was still largely on the international security agenda and the MOD was being expected to contribute towards it in a big way – action against the Taleban and al-Qaeda in Afghanistan, concern

---

10 *The Strategic Defence Review: A New Chapter*, CM 5566 (London: Stationery Office, July 2002).

about proliferation of weapons of mass destruction, and countering Saddam Hussein's perceived intentions in Iraq.

Whatever the reasons behind the MOD's rapid response, it is the case that the policies set out in that Defence Review New Chapter have continued to inform the military contribution to counter terrorism ever since and have been reiterated in successive Defence White Papers. There are four basic principles running through them all.

The first is the recognition from the outset that the battle against militant Islam cannot be won by force alone. As the Defence Secretary, Geoff Hoon, put it in his introduction to the New Chapter: the Armed Forces can only be 'just part of the Government's efforts to eliminate terrorism as a force in international affairs'.[11] It was made clear that military aspects of the response had to be integrated with a wide range of other initiatives and measures – political, diplomatic, humanitarian, financial, intelligence and law enforcement – in concert with international institutions and a wide range of other countries, some of them strange bedfellows. There was an appreciation that counter-terrorism is a long-term business, requiring roots and causes to be addressed, not just symptoms.

This view that military force is an enabler, rather than a match-winner, was inherent in defence thinking from well before 2001. 'Hearts and Minds' have been part of UK military stabilization activity since the Malaya campaign in the 1950s. In Northern Ireland, from the mid-1980s onwards, a military or coercive strategy was rejected in favour of a broader policy, whereby the Armed Forces mainly supported law enforcement in order to establish the conditions in which other measures – political, diplomatic and economic – could deliver long-term solutions. So this holistic

---

11 *Ibid.*, p. 4.

thinking, of the kind needed now, was familiar to British Armed Forces.

The second pillar of the New Chapter was the principle that the Armed Forces are more useful through action overseas rather than at home. Upstream, not downstream. As Geoff Hoon put it at the time, 'It is much better to engage our enemies in their own backyards rather than ours, at a time and place of our choosing, not theirs.'[12] The point is made still more explicitly in the New Chapter itself:

> We are not going to allow threats at home to tie up significant numbers of our high readiness armed forces and prevent us from acting abroad. If we did, those who threaten us would have won. And in any case [it goes on], our analysis shows that tackling the problems where possible at a distance is preferable to waiting for problems to come to us: in that sense operations overseas are often the best form of home defence.[13]

What the MOD had in mind was not only precisely tailored action against terrorists directly – the 'find and strike' missions against al-Qaeda in Afghanistan – but also the relevance of broader security activity of the kind the UK had engaged in successfully since the end of the Cold War to shape the international security environment, in the Balkans and in Sierra Leone. The New Chapter argues that,

> by undertaking peace support operations, usually in coalition with others, we can prevent instability or assist in stabilization. And by training other states' armed

---

12   *Ibid.*, p. 5.
13   *Ibid.*, para. 77.

forces we can transfer military skills so that they can eventually do the job for themselves. Where prevention has failed and we have engaged in coercive or destructive activities, we should be prepared to assist in post-conflict recovery, to help create the conditions for stability, thereby reducing the likelihood of the state supporting or harbouring terrorists in the future.[14]

These statements of policy – acting at a time and place of our own choosing and the apparent perceived ease of achieving post-conflict stabilization – were, of course, formulated before our experiences in Iraq and Afghanistan and may seem almost naïve now. Nevertheless, they were stated as preferences rather than assumptions about the degree of difficulty or challenge. Moreover, the proposition that a range of military operations overseas can assist in the prevention of terrorism, including actions that reduce regional instabilities or prevent the failure of states, remains one of the tenets of current official UK counter-terrorist strategy.[15] The problem is effective practical implementation, and I shall return to that later.

The third principle in the New Chapter was the conclusion that military capabilities needed to counter the new terrorist threat, broadly in line with the plans already in place to modernize British Armed Forces for expeditionary operations more generally. These had been in development since the end of the Cold War, but were defined more sharply by the Strategic Defence Review in 1998. The emphasis was already on the development of high readiness, rapid reaction forces, with the flexibility to engage in lethal operations of varying scale and intensity, together with the other military tasks of conflict

---

14   *Ibid.*, para. 16.
15   *Countering International Terrorism*, p. 28.

prevention, peace enforcement, peace keeping and aiding post-conflict reconstruction. In the words of the New Chapter, the analysis of counter-terrorist requirements set us firmly on the right track to 'reinforce the thrust of our existing plans'.[16]

It made sense, the MOD argued, to regard the planned components of UK Rapid Reaction Forces – such as improved communications, intelligence, command and control capabilities, strategic and tactical transport, campaign logistics – as being equally relevant to counter-terrorist operations. What the New Chapter did was to give added emphasis and boost to the priority associated with various equipments and concepts: so-called 'Network Enabled Capability' to harness new technology; precision-guided munitions, especially important to minimize damage to civilian populations and limit the number of weapon strikes needed; UAVs, that is Unmanned Air Vehicles or Drones, and other equipment for improved surveillance and information, again so that military objectives can be achieved with the minimum level of force; the creation through Army reorganization of an extra deployable brigade; and strengthening of Special Forces, their equipment and support.

This approach to force planning for counter-terrorism – integral to expeditionary forces as a whole rather than a separate addition – has continued to underpin MOD thinking since 2002, as set out in the subsequent White Papers of 2003 and 2004.[17] The MOD aimed to strike the right balance of capabilities across all eight of what it termed its strategic effects: to Prevent, Stabilize, Contain, Deter, Coerce, Disrupt, Defeat and Destroy.[18] It was also informed by the policy that it

---

16 'A New Chapter'; see, for example, para 92.
17 *Delivering Security in a Changing World*, CM 6041; for example, ch. 1.5 (London: Stationery Office, December 2003).
18 *Future Capabilities*, CM 6269, ch 1.2 (London: Stationery Office, July 2004).

is unwise to take a prescriptive view of how to counter international terrorism – particularly as force plans take years to mature and the world changes quickly. Since the nature of the threat could be different in different cases, the Armed Forces needed a range of capability options across a broad spectrum, able to be drawn on flexibly in response to a wide range of events.

The fourth pillar that underpins the defence counter-terrorist contribution is linked to the emphasis on operations overseas – the principle that within the UK, the responsibility lies with the Home Office and practical implementation is led by the civil agencies – police, Security Service and emergency services. The New Chapter made it clear that the Armed Forces are available to be called on for support, in various forms, and for certain specialized elements of protection at home, but set its face against the establishment of any permanent dedicated cadre in the Armed Forces for the bulk of tasks within the UK, including managing the consequences of terrorist action.

The reasons for this were partly about efficient use of resources. The Government argued – for example, in 2004 – that if planning were to 'depend critically on support from the Armed Forces, it would divert resources away from the overseas component of its counter-terrorist strategy without improving the capabilities of the civil agencies and emergency services best able to respond to contingencies in the UK'.[19]

There are also more fundamental political and indeed cultural attitudes at work in the UK, which do not always apply elsewhere. In the United States, for example, Donald Rumsfeld has announced the creation of a military force of up

---

19   Defence White Paper, 2003: 'Government Response to the Committee's Fifth Report of Session 2003–4', HC 1048 (London: Stationery Office, September 2004).

to 60,000 available for counter-terrorism at home or abroad. But in Britain there is still a deep and abiding distaste for using the military for internal security of any kind. The origins are historical, stretching back to the Glorious Revolution of 1688, and still give rise to the constitutional oddity that the MOD's budget is controlled by Parliament not just financially, through the annual budget, as with every other department, but also through explicit controls on the size of the Armed Forces, which are also enacted annually through the Defence Appropriations. You may also recall more recently the reported distress suffered by the Home Secretary, Mr Blunkett, three years ago when, for otherwise good security reasons, armoured personnel carriers were deployed at Heathrow.

However, this emphasis on the role of the Armed Forces being mainly overseas and reliance on building up civil authorities for the security task in the UK had not been going unchallenged. The House of Commons Defence Committee, led by its redoubtable chairman, Bruce George, mounted a sustained critique on this thrust of the New Chapter and the subsequent White Papers during 2003 and 2004. 'Overall', argued the Committee, 'we have seen little evidence that the MOD has taken seriously the need to rethink the capacity of the Armed Forces to provide predictable support to the task of home defence in the event of a mass-effect terrorist attack in the UK.'[20] They pressed for a rebalancing of efforts as between home and away, as well as for improved intelligence capacity and for more urgency and resources generally.

In reality these concerns had not been going unheeded within the Ministry of Defence. Those most responsible at the time (by which I mean the Secretary of State, Chief of Defence Staff and myself) also felt that the British public would not

---

20 'A New Chapter to the Strategic Defence Review: Sixth Report of Session 2002–3', HC 93-1, p. 56 (London: Stationery Office, May 2003).

understand it if there were a major crisis within the UK which swamped the civil agencies, and the Armed Forces had no planned support available or were seen to be standing idly by. For this reason, within the policy and resource parameters I have outlined, we did all possible to ensure that maximum military support would be forthcoming should the need arise.

The results of this aspect of the MOD's efforts were agreed in June 2002 and implemented over the following months. They included a variety of measures to improve military support to the civil authorities:

- Improved planning, consultation and organizational machinery to link the Armed Forces more closely with the civil authorities.
- Increased military staff for contingency and emergency planning.
- Improved communications systems between the Armed Forces, police and emergency services.
- The creation of reaction forces from the Reserves of up to 500 in each of the 14 Army brigade areas, which correspond to the system of Government Offices for the Regions and the Devolved Administrations Structure for Scotland and Wales.
- The provision of specialized forms of assistance which could not practicably be provided by the civil authorities themselves:
  - Quick reaction aircraft at high alert for interception of airborne threats.
  - Maritime counter-terrorism protection.
  - Bomb disposal, including chemical, biological and radiological devices.
  - Hostage recovery and certain Special Forces techniques.

In practice the MOD went a little further than this and the Chief of the Defence Staff took steps to ensure that any regular forces that were in the UK in the event of a major disaster would be available to help, and in a planned way.

Thankfully, little of this military support at home has been needed 'for real', so far. And the policy of increasing the capacity and budgets of the civil power – police, intelligence, emergency services – has been a considerable success. The fact that I have chosen to shed more light on the Armed Forces' role implies no criticism whatsoever of the work done by my old friends and colleagues in civil departments and organizations. And I note from a recent opinion poll that 86 per cent of the public think that the police and Security Services have performed well during the emergency Operation OVERT.[21]

There is one further way in which the MOD and military techniques have supported the development of domestic counter-terrorism and emergency planning. This is less evident to the outside world, and less tangible, but possibly more significant. It concerns the transfer of crisis management skills from defence to civil departments. Among the best features of the UK Armed Forces is their ability to combine two very different sorts of disciplines into their way of working, part of their basic training and upbringing. One is the habit of meticulous advance planning for contingencies, which is underpinned in detail by scenario testing, doctrine development, regular exercising and the like. The other is the capacity for rapid and flexible decision-making in a crisis, with the ability to change plans rapidly as circumstances dictate. Blending the two together is what enables them to act and deliver results so effectively in practice.

Detailed analysis of this operational ethos would merit a

---

21   YouGov poll published in the *Daily Telegraph*, 25 August 2006.

lecture in itself. But it is sufficient for my purpose here to say that transfer of these techniques and skills to civil departments has occurred over the past five years or so. This has been partly through the lessons learned from military support in crises such as foot-and-mouth in 2000/2001 and partly through the transfer of personnel, both military and civilian, from the MOD to Cabinet Office units and elsewhere. It is no coincidence that the two leading figures in co-ordinating UK counter-terrorist effort – David Omand and Richard Mottram – both came from distinguished careers in the Ministry of Defence. Moreover, defence officials carry out much of the underpinning work in the Cabinet Office as well as participating fully in the central intelligence unit within the Security Service, the Joint Terrorist Analysis Centre.

But I need to return to my main theme. Despite their important contribution to home security, the principal role of the Armed Forces in counter-terrorism remains the operations undertaken overseas – what I have called the upstream element.

To date, these operations cannot be said to have reduced the threat we face.

- On Iraq, Western opinion remains polarized. The French Socialist presidential favourite, Segolene Royal, claimed in a widely reported remark in August 2006: 'Preventative wars aggravate the problems they presume to tackle.'
- In a recent UK opinion poll[22] a clear majority of those canvassed believed that British policy significantly increased the risk of terrorist attack in the UK, and that this risk would be decreased if we changed our foreign policy, distanced ourselves from America, were more critical of Israel and declared a timetable for withdrawal from Iraq.

---

22   Opinion poll in *The Times*, 6 September 2006.

- The editor of the London-based newspaper *Al-Quds al-Arabi* claims that 'the situation in Iraq more than anything has provided al-Qaeda with a safe haven and endless hordes of fighters eager to die opposing the US occupation of their country'.[23]

But if the thrust of these arguments is that basic foreign policies have to change if terrorism is to be overcome, that option is clearly rejected by coalition governments, led by the US and UK. And the reasons for this are substantive and go to the heart of the matter. It is not just the basic unacceptability of 'giving in' to terrorism.

Even if there were to be a withdrawal from Iraq, there is no reason to believe that this would put an end to Islamic terrorism. The causes stem from more fundamental differences than that, as evidenced by the fact that 9/11 and other atrocities pre-dated the coalition action in 2003. Interestingly, in *The Times*' poll I mentioned, where respondents linked government policy to the risk of terrorist attack, nearly two-thirds of them also believed that even if British foreign policy were different, Muslim extremists would still find another excuse for terrorist activity, 'such is their hatred of democracy and the Western way of life'.[24]

Governments also stand on the position that their foreign policy cannot be decided and determined by the perceived effects on Muslim opinion, should this clash with what they believe to be right, whether over Iraq, support for evolutionary reform rather than violent change in countries such as Saudi Arabia and Egypt, support for Israel's right to exist, or, indeed, support for the Afghan Government in their renewed struggle

---

23   Abdel Bari Atwan, *The Secret History of Al Qa'ida* (London: Saqi Books, 2006), p. 236.
24   Opinion poll in *The Times*, 6 September 2006.

against the Taliban. Nor, for that matter, looking to the future, could our politicians afford to sit idly by and allow Iran to develop its plans and policies, including her nuclear ambitions, unchecked.

So what, in these circumstances, and in the light of the considerations I have outlined, is a successful counter-terrorist strategy likely to require, and what should be the role of military force within it?

We do, of course, have our strategy for the UK in the White Paper. My point is that this has to be combined more fully with the foreign policy and overseas security dimension.

It is certainly not my purpose here to argue for a fundamental change in our foreign policy. At the same time, it is difficult to maintain the position that existing policy has had no effect on terrorism, even if it is not the fundamental causation. Therefore, the first element in a fuller strategy – 'joining up the dots', as I describe it in my title – has to focus on foreign policy, in the context of reducing the support, sympathy or tolerance for terrorism in various quarters. If progress is to be made, there will have to be active recognition of the need to address legitimate grievances where they exist, and to do so through convincing engagement. This raises issues well beyond the scope of this lecture and is about the role of the United States and Europe, not just the UK itself. Measures such as the Prime Minister's attempt to breathe life back into the Middle East peace process are important elements, as is the need for the international community as a whole to put across to moderate Muslim opinion the true reasons for our presence in Iraq and Afghanistan.

But when so much of the terrorist agenda is not about territorial grievances which could conceivably be addressed by negotiation, but about basic values and methods of pursuing them, on which there cannot be a compromise, it seems inevitable that our Armed Forces will continue to be needed overseas, preferably supporting broad coalition and UN efforts, just as our security forces are needed at home.

Iraq is clearly the wrong model in a number of respects. As regards the justification for the coalition action in the first place, views remain polarized and I do not propose to get into that except to observe that while preventative wars, as Segolene Royal puts it, are fraught with problems, governments still have to resolve the question of what is to be done to protect society in circumstances where deterrence or containment has failed and there is intelligence of hostile intention. It is not sufficient to argue that the answer is to wait until perfect knowledge is available, because then it could be too late.

As regards the way in which military force was actually employed in Iraq, was it that we lacked the right concepts or failed to move on from the Cold War? General Sir Rupert Smith suggests as much in his book, when he writes as follows: 'The people', he writes, 'are not the enemy, the enemy is amongst the people, and the purpose of any use of military force and other power is to differentiate between the enemy and the people and win the latter over to you.'[25] But this is the very doctrine that I heard from our Chiefs of Staff through seven years' close association with them. As is evident from our New Chapter to the Strategic Defence Review that I have cited, the need for military force to be applied selectively and as only one element in a comprehensive policy plan is firmly entrenched in British thinking. But, of course, it was not the same elsewhere.

While there were detailed plans for the use of military force, which went through countless iterations, they were not part, from the outset, of an overarching policy plan designed, to put it simply, to win the peace. It was the policy plan, familiar to the Foreign Office or the State Department, that was lacking, not the military one. As is now well known, the need was for a

25   R. Smith, *The Utility of Force*, p. 396.

security framework to be put in place quickly, within which confidence could be restored and economic and political reconstruction could take place.

In major parts of Iraq the coalition's initial military success was not followed fast enough by the other necessary elements, whether in terms of the availability of sufficient forces to provide the security framework, creation of an Iraqi-led administration including internal security forces, or by arrival of the resources necessary for reconstruction. None of this would have been easy and I do not propose to go into the detail of why and how vital time was lost. It requires a separate analysis of the inter-agency views, debate and process within Washington and London, as well as of developments in Iraq. As it was, a vacuum emerged in which sectarian conflict, insurgency and terrorism was able to expand and grow.

The need for more integrated policies to underpin military intervention and dynamic planning for post-conflict reconstruction – beginning well before military action takes place – are much better understood in the light of this experience. But I suspect there is some way to go as far as the international community as a whole is concerned in putting this into practical effect.

This is not an academic observation. Similarly integrated approaches also need to be applied by NATO now in Afghanistan. Success in the three campaigns under way – stabilization activity, the counter-terrorist campaign and support for the Afghan Government's anti-narcotics campaign – may well depend on the ability of NATO and the Afghan Government to combine all of these elements into a comprehensive and flexible policy, including provision for alternative livelihoods for the people denied poppy cultivation; success is unlikely to be achieved if they are pursued separately as individual operations without taking account of the effect of one campaign on the others.

But as I suggested earlier, some more traditional concepts about the use of military force are also relevant to today's challenges. It is a long-standing principle that when agreed military operations are embarked on, there need to be sufficient forces to perform the task as quickly as possible, to prevent drawn-out campaigns which alienate the local population and to provide continuing security after any war-fighting phase. This says something about the size of the Armed Forces that the UK needs to sustain in its national force planning. It also says a lot about the need for adequate burden-sharing between contributing nations.

NATO's history and success were based on such burden-sharing principles. Today there is political unity over what is at stake in Afghanistan, but this is not, apparently, yet matched by a similar unity of purpose in providing the military forces of the right type and quality, particularly in Helmand province, to combat the Taleban insurgency. Those of us involved in planning for the UK to take the lead in that operation recognized at the time that success would depend on other countries being prepared to pull their weight too. The Danish and Canadian forces are, I know, doing everything that could be expected of them, but there is plenty of room, and need, for others to do more.

It is often said that what is needed for the UK to position itself better in countering international terrorism is to distance ourselves further from US policy. I would argue to the contrary, and based on our history, values and global interests, that the need is to foster closer international co-operation at all levels – intelligence, foreign policy, aid policy, law enforcement, as well as military solidarity. And to do so with the focus on the development of a new transatlantic bargain to deal with twenty-first-century security challenges. It took NATO 20 years from its inception to the achievement of a fully integrated strategy, known as MC 14/3, based on the doctrine of forward defence and flexible response. The present challenges are more complex, less monolithic, less about states, and the response needs to be geared accordingly in a suitably differentiated way. But we do not have 20 years in which to arrive at a similarly agreed, united and sustained approach.

To conclude. We cannot afford to ignore the role to be played by the Armed Forces in counter-terrorist strategy. Although the nature of terrorism has changed, military force is still needed, to support the emergency and security services at home and to act abroad, both in direct combat, where essential, and as part of wider stabilization efforts. The overseas dimension will remain critical. Much will, however, depend on the ability of the UK and its allies to agree on strategies that are based on clear foreign policy objectives and in which direct military action against terrorism is combined with security and practical measures of assistance that manifestly improve the lives of peoples in the affected regions. Military force can succeed as an integral element in dynamic plans which incorporate the necessary political, civil and economic dimensions, but not if used separately or as a substitute for them.

The test of whether this more integrated security concept is translated into practical effect will depend, in the UK at least, on whether the existing machinery of government is changed to meet the new challenges; in terms of some adjustment of departmental boundaries as between Defence, Foreign and Commonwealth Office, Department for International Development and Home Office, their relevant budgetary arrangements and in the creation of a stronger central co-ordinating capacity in the Cabinet Office area. But that needs to be the subject of a further paper.

5

Reflections on
Secret Intelligence[1]

David Omand

The occasion of the annual Peter Nailor Lecture at Gresham College in 2005 was an opportunity to reflect on my recent experience, as UK Security and Intelligence Co-ordinator, the first holder of that Permanent Secretary post in the Cabinet Office taking on the traditional responsibilities of the Cabinet Secretary for intelligence and security matters. My post brought together for the first time responsibility as Accounting Officer for the three secret intelligence agencies and thus for thinking about their future development, organization and funding, with the operational responsibility for central crisis management. In a way that is characteristic of the evolutionary British approach to institution building, this construct then allowed me to use the role to develop strategic thinking on counter-terrorism, including pulling together in a British context what our American colleagues call 'homeland security' and what in the context of this book we might call 'the protective state'. The value of having a full-time senior official at the centre of the overlapping circles of intelligence, security, homeland security and crisis management is, I hope, now evident. The Government has now completed this phase of

---

1 This chapter is a lightly edited version of the 2005 Nailor Lecture at Gresham College, in the City of London.

evolutionary development by giving the Security and Intelligence Co-ordinator also the responsibility of chairing the Joint Intelligence Committee. The UK has therefore for the first time in its history a single senior official at the top of the British intelligence community in its widest sense, demonstrating once again that the shortest distance between two points in governmental space is not necessarily a straight line. But more of all that in a moment.

This chapter is organized into three linked sections, which cannot hope to be comprehensive but may give an insight into some of the issues.

First, the purposes of intelligence. I shall reflect on the past and future uses of intelligence, and its inherent limitations. What purposes does it serve today and how important will it really be for supporting 'the protective state'?

Second, the meaning of intelligence. The title of this chapter deliberately echoes the title of the memoir by the late Professor R. V. Jones[2] who did so much to develop scientific intelligence during World War II. His writings contain encouraging and practical lessons for those in the intelligence community – and for those they serve – and I shall return below to some of these in asking how we can best apply modern scientific method in assessing intelligence for public protection. Why do we often get it right but nevertheless sometimes get it very wrong?

Third, the evolution of the intelligence community. What factors should shape future organization, particularly in the face of the threat from international terrorism? Are there lessons we should learn from the history of the central organization for defence over the last 60 years? Are there principles that are internationally applicable?

---

2   R. V. Jones, *Reflections on Secret Intelligence* (London: Mandarin, 1989).

1. The purpose that intelligence serves

A starting definition might be that the ultimate object of intelligence is to enable action to be optimized by reducing ignorance; and of secret intelligence to achieve this objective in respect of information that others wish to remain hidden. Thus stated, the purpose of intelligence is not linked simply to knowledge for its own sake but to organized information that can be put to use. The military commander and the policy-maker alike need to have professional staff support to collect and organize information relevant to the decisions and actions that they want to take, and some that they may not yet know they need to take.

Intelligence provides, therefore, in the words of the 2004 Australian intelligence commission:

- Warning, notably of terrorist plans, but also of potential conflicts, uprisings and coups.
- Understanding of the regional and international environment with which decision-makers will need to grapple.
- Knowledge of the military capabilities and intentions of potential adversaries, a vital ingredient in defence procurement and preparedness.
- Support for military operations, minimizing casualties and improving the environment for operational success.
- Support for an active and ambitious foreign, trade and defence policy.
- And beyond these vital roles of intelligence in providing information, modern intelligence can be a more active tool of government – disrupting the plans of adversaries, influencing the policies of key foreign actors and contributing to modern electronic warfare.[3]

---

3   P. Flood, *Report of the Inquiry into Australian Intelligence Agencies* (Canberra: Government of Australia, 2004).

The greatest added value of the secret part of intelligence comes, as Lord Butler emphasized in his report on intelligence into weapons of mass destruction (WMD),[4] because for many of the topics of most pressing interest there are active measures employed against us designed to hide or disguise the information we seek. So traditional secret intelligence from human sources, from intercepted communications, from electronic or other measurements, from analysis of acquired enemy equipment, from defectors and from satellite reconnaissance, has a unique value. The intelligence analyst has also always drawn on diplomatic reporting, and increasingly open sources of all kinds and in the future increasingly on patterns drawn from data mining of large sets of data, both open and protected. Open sources are important, not least because secret intelligence is also expensive to collect and process, and unnecessary reliance on secret sources is wasteful. But I deliberately start with purpose and use, rather than sources and methods, to point us towards the recognition that in the future we shall need to put proportionally more national effort into collation, analysis, assessment and research than in the immediate past. And hence my earlier reference to the need to think of a British intelligence community that is wider than just the three main Secret Agencies. When it is all put together, the test of effectiveness of the overall community is how far it can genuinely help reduce ignorance in each of the areas I listed, meeting the different needs of an increasingly diverse set of non-traditional as well as traditional customers.

Is this broad definition so very different, then, from the craft of journalism? The view of *The Economist* magazine is worth repeating on this point. In a comment in 1966 on the retirement of Sir Kenneth Strong as MOD Director General of

4   R. Butler, *Review of Intelligence on Weapons of Mass Destruction* (London: House of Commons, HC 898, 2004).

Intelligence, *The Economist* wrote: 'Modern intelligence has to do with the painstaking collection and analysis of fact, the exercise of judgement, and clear and quick presentation. It is not simply what serious journalists would always produce if they had time: it is something more rigorous, continuous, and above all operational – that is to say, related to something that somebody wants to do or may be forced to do.'

'More rigorous, continuous and above all operational': continuity is certainly important. I recall during the Falklands campaign the frantic search by the analysts for information about the Port Stanley runway whose size was crucial to assessments of Argentine capability but which had recently been upgraded. The information did not involve secret intelligence; the extra hard-standing had been paid for by the British taxpayer as a civil development project but had never found its way onto the defence intelligence database, no doubt because too few people were trying to keep up with too much information. A very different, and much more serious, example was well dramatized by Robert Harris in his novel *Enigma*,[5] vividly illustrating the high stakes when continuity is lost, in that case in signals intelligence on submarine movements during the Battle of the Atlantic. Continuity of the overall information base is an essential, if sometimes unglamorous, role for the intelligence staffs for which resources have to be found. Increasingly, with pressure on staff numbers in customer departments, it is a function that the wider intelligence community may have to fulfil on behalf of government.

Behind continuity in assessment lies continuing availability of sources. Building capability takes time, in recruiting and training, and in researching, developing and building technical systems. The risks of failure to recognize this can be serious. In 1844 after the Mazzini affair, over-zealous parliamentary

---

5   R. Harris, *Enigma* (London: Arrow, 1996).

committees of inquiry led to the abolition of the Secret Office and the Decyphering Branch, which had been serving British interests since it opened in 1653 and was put on a legal footing by Parliament in 1670. As a result, Britain entered World War I without an effective Sigint (signals intelligence) system, which had rapidly to be assembled from scratch in Room 40 in the Old Admiralty Building to help fight the war at sea and the German submarine campaign. 'Gentlemen do not read each other's mail', said US Secretary Stimson in 1931, in an excess of ethical foreign policy that meant after Pearl Harbor the US went to war comparably handicapped.

Those past gaps in continuity were caused by qualms over the acceptability of the methods of secret intelligence. Gaps in continuity of a different kind could occur in future, with even more direct consequences for public safety, if doubts are not allayed about the use of modern IT and data-processing by the intelligence agencies in their counter-terrorist campaigns. The proposals recently before the European Parliament for the retention of communications data are a case in point. But all our experience of fighting terrorism in the past shows that where pre-emptive intelligence is available, effective action to protect the public can be taken with minimum disruption to the community and without having to contemplate serious distortion of the rule of law, in effect allowing in respect of state coercion the bludgeon to be exchanged for the rapier.

Of necessity, the methods for uncovering terrorist or criminal networks and support structures depend upon the opponents having only imperfect knowledge of them. So a fully informed public debate about intelligence methods is hard to have. Trust is needed, for example if governments put forward a case for limiting data protection, that such limitation of privacy will really represent a higher degree of assurance of greater security or reduce the temptation to dilute the due processes of criminal justice. So it is vital that there is public trust in the integrity of those serving in the secret world, including that they will follow what R. V. Jones called the doctrine of 'minimum necessary trespass' into privacy, in a parallel with the doctrine of 'minimum necessary force' that is enshrined in our common law. I discuss these issues further in Chapter 7.

When he was US Director of Central Intelligence, Stansfield Turner expressed this question of public justification of intelligence methods thus: 'There is one overall test of the ethics of human intelligence activities. That is whether those approving them feel they could defend their decisions before the public if their actions became public.' He qualified this remark by saying that he was not advocating a prior consideration of what the public would stand in terms of assessing the public mood at the particular moment of decision; but he was advocating the combination of readiness to stand up and be counted if exposure came, with personal conviction of the rationale you would then deploy. Implicitly, what under that doctrine is never justifiable would be to undertake activities that you would be ashamed to try and defend, and which therefore rely only on the cloak of secrecy remaining intact.

The quote from *The Economist* also referred to the operational purpose of intelligence. In recent times there has been a major increase in the relative importance of intelligence for 'action this day', particularly in the areas of countering terrorism, proliferation, narcotics and serious crime, as against intelligence to inform policy-making. And who can be surprised? Recent terrorist attacks have, for example, illustrated starkly the need for pre-emptive intelligence, just as the previous successes in disrupting terrorist cells planning to attack the UK and our interests abroad showed that good intelligence saves lives.

In reflecting on the purposes of intelligence, I find it helpful to think of the intelligence community serving three levels:

these are the classic distinctions between working at the strategic level (including what Churchill called grand strategy), at the operational level and at the tactical level, with the main distinguishing feature between the levels being the time horizon of the customers receiving the intelligence. These distinctions can be a helpful guide – for example, when it comes to evolve organizations able to operate at each level and when it comes to building the right institutions and liaisons internationally.

At the *strategic* level, intelligence assessments might, for example, look at the future evolution of terrorist movements, or countries at risk of instability or the possibility of conflicts over global trends in energy supplies or water resources – all issues where the horizon is years or decades ahead. This is the everyday diet of the Joint Intelligence Committee, supported by expert Current Intelligence Groups, in which senior policy-makers and intelligence chiefs try to arrive at joint key judgements on the evolution of issues where there are important national interests in security, defence and foreign affairs. Some scepticism is healthy: rarely could it have been said that secret intelligence was the decisive factor in policy-making itself. And in the policy arena we have what W. W. Rostow called, in relation to the 1944 controversy over the effectiveness of the aerial bombing campaign, 'the arena of power, vested interest and personality where forces quite different from straightforward intellectual argument were at work'. In my personal experience, however, from my years serving in the defence and security world, better, sometimes much better, outcomes have resulted from applying secret intelligence in the relevant fields than would otherwise have been the case – for example, as Lord Butler confirmed, in the successes in countering proliferation in relation to Libya, Iran, North Korea and from the AQ Khan network.

At the *operational* level, the main demand is for timely all-source analysis to support operational decision-making:

examples might be over the risks to a military deployment, or the threat to an Embassy overseas threatened by terrorists, or the implications of high-tech weaponry reaching a country of concern, or whether a particular export of specialized steels should be permitted, or additional protective security measures taken at a big public event or on a transport system. The intelligence community provides professional judgements on which it is for the policy community, and in major cases ultimately ministers, to decide whether and how to act. The policy-makers have to accept the assessments as they stand, as they do with military, medical or legal opinions. They know that they will be hammered, however unfairly, by the media if things go wrong and if they appear to have ignored warnings – or the opposite, to have pressed on despite cautious assessments. So the analysts in practice have leverage. They need to be sensitive to the dangers. By playing too safe themselves and passing on the problem, they may make it harder for the right risk-management judgements to be taken, leading to over-restrictive security measures or warning fatigue leading to complacency. We should have sympathy with those who have to make these assessments, and encourage them to remain true to the principles of rational evidence-based judgement.

At the *tactical* level, individual lines of intelligence are largely going raw to other intelligence specialists – for example, supporting the front-line work of the military, the police, the Intelligence Agencies themselves and to defence staffs or Whitehall customers who are themselves sufficiently expert to be able to interpret the material. Systems for analysis and rapid distribution are increasingly available to support operations on the ground – for example, the tactical application of intelligence to guide a counter-terrorist raid, or to follow a drugs shipment, or to intercept a breach of sanctions. This is the part of the iceberg of which the public rarely is conscious, unless things go awry.

Lord Butler also correctly drew attention to the penumbra of uncertainty that usually surround the fragments of intelligence that become available. Given the inevitable imperfections and gaps in the intelligence, what is required from an officer concerned with the assessment of intelligence at each of these three levels is, as Clausewitz wrote 200 years ago and Lord Butler cited, 'a certain degree of discrimination, which can only be gained from knowledge of men and affairs and from good judgement. The law of probability must be his guide.'

2. Divining the meaning of intelligence

That reference to probability is an appropriate cue to move on to consider how meaning can best be derived from intelligence.

The Joint Intelligence Committee (or JIC) has for the past 70 years had the responsibility of producing predictive strategic judgements for the highest levels of British government. The JIC process is, as far as I know, unique around the world. One reason may be that the Committee has as members not only the heads of the UK intelligence community but also the key Whitehall senior policy officials, including from the Cabinet Office, Foreign and Commonwealth Office (FCO), Defence, Home Office, HM Treasury, and Trade and Industry. The process of assessment therefore involves close interaction between the professional intelligence community and the senior policy-makers, examining the most sensitive intelligence in the course of producing JIC papers. All have to dip their hands in the blood of the collective judgements, however unwelcome they may be.

The reason the JIC emerged during World War II as it did was to bring greater rationality into bitter strategic policy debate. Take the exchange in 1934 as Vansittart, Head of the Diplomatic Service, read what he saw as – Treasury-inspired

– complacent air ministry estimates of German war production: 'In any case, prophecy is largely a matter of imagination. I do not think that the Service Departments have enough. On the other hand, they might say that we [that is, the Foreign Office and the Secret Intelligence Service] have too much. The answer is perhaps that we know the Germans better.' Air Marshal Sir Victor Goddard from the Air Ministry, on the other hand, minuted, 'What passes for intelligence of the enemy's intentions is more usually propaganda for a change of Government policy: honest propaganda, maybe, but based on ideas rather than facts.' After seven years' service on the JIC, in three different posts, I am convinced of the advantages of bringing intelligence chiefs and senior policy-makers together for an afternoon every week to debate the evidence on the issues of the day and hammer out a collective judgement. I am encouraged in this by the fact that Lord Butler's committee of inquiry looked for but found no evidence of cross-contamination in the JIC between policy and assessment. So the principle is right, but of course that is not to say that the practice is always perfect, which is why it is important that Lord Butler's recommendations for improving the process remain fresh in mind.

The professionals' task is therefore to keep judgements anchored to what the intelligence actually reveals (or does not reveal) and keep in check any predisposition of policy-makers to pontificate – that being the practice, as described by Norman Dixon[6] – of trying to make nasty facts go away by the magical process of emitting loud noises in the opposite direction. The policy-makers in turn ensure that the judgements actually try to address the issues that need answering rather than just those on which their intelligence sources are richest, and help the professionals couch any warnings justified by the

---

6   N. Dixon, *On The Psychology of Military Incompetence* (London: Vintage Pimlico, 1994).

intelligence, without their seeming to attack the policy itself and thus risk compromising the neutrality of the JIC. This is not always easy. President Reagan is quoted by Robert Gates,[7] later Director of Central Intelligence, as complaining about these intelligence guys:

> When I was growing up in Texas, we had a cow named Bessie. One day I'd worked hard and gotten a full pail of milk, but I wasn't paying attention and old Bessie swung her shit-smeared tail through that bucket of milk. Now, you know, that's what those intelligence guys do. You work hard and get a good programme or policy going, and they swing a shit-smeared tail through it.

So speaking truth unto power is not going to guarantee popularity. But the message to those in power has to be follow what R. V. Jones quoted as Crow's law: 'Do not believe what you want to believe until you know what you ought to know.'

Forcing these top, and very busy, officials to work actively together in the JIC on key judgements for an afternoon every week of the year generates a sense of political–military community that is uniquely well informed about each other and that has very high levels of mutual understanding and trust. That is, for example, one reason why intelligence and government officials in the UK have been able to work across boundaries on counter-terrorism in ways that most nations with their more compartmented traditions have not yet achieved.

Unlike in Washington, there has never been in the UK the tradition of daily personal intelligence briefings for the Prime Minister, or an elaborate Daily Briefing Book whose compilation became such a major load for the CIA Director and now

---

7   R. M. Gates, *From the Shadows* (New York: Simon and Schuster, 1996).

for the new Director of National Intelligence. In his memoirs,[8] Zbigniew Brzezinski, National Security Adviser to President Carter, admits that he excluded Stansfield Turner, the CIA Director, and his intelligence analysts from the morning presidential briefings because he wanted the meetings to be policy- not intelligence-focused. The right instinct, but as we were reminded by Lord Justice Scott some years ago, it is potentially dangerous to have intelligence material being interpreted without the intelligence experts having the opportunity to comment on whether it will bear the weight the policy-makers might like. Winston Churchill, on the other hand, after criticizing the JIC in 1941 for its slowness in reporting that Germany would be prepared to attack Russia, wrote, 'I had not been content for this form of collective wisdom, and preferred to see the originals (agents' reports, decrypts, etc.) myself . . . thus forming my own opinions, sometimes at much earlier dates.' Prime ministers making their own assessment of raw intelligence has, of course, fallen out of fashion since. Secret intelligence with its glimpses of sources and methods is certainly more interesting than much that passes over the senior desk and can become addictive. I think that the British system now operating, with the JIC Chairman and his central analysts sending in briefly assessed highlights from the intelligence that has come in overnight, illuminating urgent or current business, backed up by more formal JIC assessment and meetings when needed, does avoid descent into the tactical and the risk of rush to judgement on the basis of what may be only a fragment of intelligence.

At the JIC level, judgements often have to concern mysteries as well as secrets, using R. V. Jones' helpful distinction between that which can in principle be known through secret intelligence, and predictions, mysteries that have to be divined,

---

8   Z. Brzezinski, *Power and Principle* (London: Weidenfeld and Nicolson, 1983).

such as what dictators might do in circumstances yet to arise. The advantage of getting the JIC to tackle such mysteries is that there is a great deal of experience to bring to bear, and a structured process with checks and balances. The risk is that speculative judgements may be taken as resting on more intelligence than they actually are, or are being over-interpreted through application of what R. V. Jones labels 'Crabtree's bludgeon': 'No set of mutually inconsistent observations can exist for which some human intellect cannot conceive a coherent explanation, however contrived.' The best practice is, as Lord Butler's Committee recognized, to ensure that the form and language of assessments is clear and explicit about the limitations of the material on which judgements rest.

Lord Butler also helpfully supported a more professional approach to the career development and training of the wider community of analysts throughout government. Part of this must be the development of assessment methodology to be applied across the community. It was 50 years before Clausewitz wrote about obeying the laws of probability that the Revd Thomas Bayes in his 'Essay towards solving a Problem in the Doctrine of Chances' provided the rule to enable posterior knowledge to be brought to bear to revise the probability of an event. For example, the likelihood of a judgement being true can be revised on receipt of a new, apparently confirmatory, intelligence report by multiplying the conditional probability of the judgement being correct (assuming the information in the new report is actually true) by the probability that the piece of evidence in the new report itself is true. One practical lesson here for those directing intelligence operations is that if you only go looking for positive evidence of a proposition, the probability of finding something in that category is rather high and therefore a spurious additional weight can be given to the relevant judgements. Intelligence officers have to be constantly on the watch for the inductivist fallacy, and set out consciously to keep testing the negative hypothesis rather than just build up information that confirms the prevailing wisdom.

I have therefore always seen a parallel with the explanatory nature of scientific theory. The value of a strategic intelligence judgement, like a scientific theory, lies in its explanatory power, and thus its predictive power. But all scientific explanations – that is, scientific theories – are provisional and open to revision. So, similarly, successive intelligence assessments are liable to change as new intelligence becomes available, which does not make those who wrote them ignorant or knaves. Following R. V. Jones, a course in modern scientific method should be compulsory not just for those who analyse and use intelligence but for those who write about it.

Of course, there are many ways in which we can still get it wrong. Intelligence is rarely evidence. For example, the true signal can get lost in the noise. To cite the eighteenth-century Revd Bayes again, 'The more observations you make with an imperfect instrument, the more certain it seems to be that the error in your conclusion will be proportional to the imperfection of the instrument made use of.' Perhaps, for example, the error came from information that was deliberately intended to deceive us, a perennial problem that R. V. Jones addressed: in any channel of intelligence in which you may be deceived – and I would add 'or whose interpretation is crucial' – work down to a greater level of sophistication than the opponent has expected you to adopt, and bring to bear all possible channels of intelligence to check for consistency.

Another source of error may be that the information on which the model is based is no longer current. This leads to the inevitable distortions of predicting the road ahead from looking into the rear-view mirror. And the relationship between analyst and customer is part of the equation. For example, predicting discontinuity could be held to be better for the analyst when matters are genuinely uncertain. If you are right, that is great. If wrong, there are any number of plausible reasons why the revolution or whatever might not have happened as predicted. But go the other way, and you are wrong and government is caught on the hop, then the stigma of 'intelligence failure' will be thrown at you. And in what Professor Adams of University College London calls 'bottom loop' bias in risk management, these uncomfortable experiences tend to stay with us, and affect our internal perceptions of risk. Fear of failure is a powerful motivator, and the more senior you are the further you have to fall, as Norman Dixon pointed out many years ago in relation to military commanders. Analysts, in my experience, know the traps, although sometimes may lean too far over to avoid them, and over the years the JIC has probably been more often wrong by under- rather than over-estimating the pace of change in overseas regimes. Mirror-imaging is a familiar phenomenon, and R. V. Jones gives examples from the world of scientific intelligence. But it is also hard for civilized, often gentle souls engaged in rational analysis to credit the effrontery of a dictator, as a re-reading of the Franks Report on the origins of the Falklands conflict will remind us.

We may find therefore that prediction does not match reality because the model of human motivation being used in interpreting the intelligence rests on inappropriate (and probably unrecognized) assumptions. Let me adapt a parable attributed to Bertrand Russell in his philosophy lectures and quoted by the Oxford physicist David Deutsch[9] to illustrate this aspect of the nature of explanation. Imagine a chicken farm, where the chickens carry out an espionage operation on the farmer and intercept a message that he is ordering much more chicken food. The JIC of chickens meets. Is their key judgement to be that at last peaceful coexistence has come and

9   D. Deutsch, *The Fabric of Reality* (London: Penguin Books, 1997).

the farmer is going to feed them properly in the future? Or is it that they are all doomed since they are about to be fattened for the kill? Two diametrically opposing key judgements that could be based on the same intelligence report. The choice of explanation may indeed rest on prior, often implicit, assumptions about human behaviour, not on the intelligence itself.

It is part of the burden of command that decisions sometimes have to be taken quickly on the basis of fragmentary evidence. An unexpected fact is less easily absorbed than one that is already expected. So even where the intelligence is not sufficiently compelling to provide detailed answers, the very process of analysis can be helpful. The timing of the 2005 terrorist attacks in the UK may have come as a tactical shock because of absence of pre-emptive intelligence, but were not seen as a strategic surprise either in terms of method, target, or the background of those involved. Intelligence assessment had highlighted the need to prepare for exactly such an eventuality, and that thankfully had been absorbed, and the response on the day was swift and highly effective.

To these problems for the analyst must then be added the potential effect of cognitive dissonance on the part of the customer for intelligence, when a person comes to be given knowledge or possesses beliefs which conflict with a decision he has made. Once a key decision has been made, and Norman Dixon has some good military examples, the psychological situation of the decision-taker can change decisively. The historical experience is that there is a tendency then for less emphasis on objectivity, and more partiality and bias in the way that the decision-taker views and evaluates the alternatives.

A question R. V. Jones raised from his World War II experience is whether in those circumstances it is legitimate for the analyst to resort to advocacy rather than present facts neutrally if they fear their warnings are not being heeded. PowerPoint is now the norm, and even the military commander can quickly summon up charts, graphs and statistics for the visiting minister. Who could blame an analyst for advocacy faced with, say, a General Percival in Singapore refusing to accept the reality of the impending Japanese invasion? Or a Secretary of Defense, as Robert McNamara admits in his own memoir,[10] resisting appreciation of the true state of affairs developing in Vietnam? R. V. Jones himself confesses to such lapses into advocacy on two occasions. But, as he warns, this must never, ever, become the slanting of intelligence. The customer has to recognize that what the analyst is painting is an impressionist portrait, without the complete detail that you would find in a photograph. So what is included as the essential highlights and what is left out as distracting detail is a matter of analytical judgement. Customer and analyst alike need to be conscious of this.

3. The future form of the UK intelligence community

The organization of a national intelligence community is never going to be simple since, as R. V. Jones remarked, input is by source and output is by subject.

There are precedents for tackling organizational problems with such characteristics. I was involved in the mid-1980s and again in the 1990s in redesigning the central organization for defence. We had to tackle the dilemma of reconciling the existence of separate services – Royal Navy, Army and Royal Air Force – with the joint nature of planning and investment in, and ultimately the generation of, military power. The failed Canadian attempt in the 1980s to combine their services shows the penalties of ignoring the different characteristics of each service, adapted to their sea, land or air environment, and

---

10   R. S. McNamara, *In Retrospect: the Tragedy and Lessons of Vietnam* (New York: Random House, 1995).

the part that their traditions play in maintaining operational effectiveness and recruiting alike. Equally, once they reached a senior level, as Sir Ian Jacob and Lord Ismay had noted as early as 1963, based on their deep wartime experience, officers had to train and work together to develop the best defence answer, and there had to be a Chief of Defence Staff with authority to give a 'purple' perspective. And we could not afford the inefficiency, waste and military ineffectiveness of having separate procurement, repair, supply and logistic chains, and separate IT and communications systems, let alone separate operational planning (a lesson should have been clear to Britain at least since the 1911 Agadir crisis).

My approach to such issues has been to look on organizations not as machinery described by lines on charts, but as adaptive organisms, evolving over time to try to fit their environment. Changes that are seen to be going with the grain of history tend to produce longer-lasting results than the discontinuities introduced by sudden changes of direction. The law of unexpected consequences tends to apply to short-cuts. The words of the Duke of Cambridge, whose statue stands outside the Old War Office, hover in the air: 'There is a time for everything, and the time for change is when you can no longer help it.' But we do not normally have the time to wait for such realization of inevitability to dawn unaided on the staffs. So to accelerate the process, we need to show that the necessary changes fit a narrative that explains convincingly where the institution has been, how it is evolving and why the time has come to accelerate the pace of change. And after the Falklands campaign, as the Principal Private Secretary to the Secretary of State, John Nott, in MOD, I was certainly convinced that if the mission is defence, then the watchword had better be organize for war and adapt for peace rather than the other way round. That 1980s MOD reorganization was rightly presented as further steps in accelerating an evolutionary process that had been under way for generations. Indeed, I recall being delighted to find the main line of development anticipated in the Lord Esher's Report of the War Office Reconstruction Committee of 1904.

Can we similarly discern what Professor Hennessy calls 'the thin wisps of tomorrow', in Braudel's phrase, in the evolution of organization for secret intelligence?

It is not hard to spot what going with the grain might involve:

- Intelligence in its widest sense is more than ever needed to reduce ignorance and encourage rational decision-taking, given the changes taking place in the world.
- Without secret intelligence we will not understand sufficiently the nature of some important threats that face us.
- But open sources are also becoming relatively more important and need more investment so that we have a rounded intelligence picture.
- Increasingly, tasks of research, analysis and assessment, and strategic warning, are falling to the wider intelligence community.
- The community is serving a wider group of customers; they are rightly demanding rapid and secure access to intelligence in all its forms, and expect it to be cross-referred, collated, assessed and distributed and for rapid agreement to be given to its use for action.
- Differing demands arise for supporting the strategic, operational and tactical levels, and different considerations apply for establishing the most effective international links at each of these levels.
- The modern threats of international terrorism, transnational crime and proliferation have led to blurring of distinctions between home and overseas theatres of operations; agencies must work easily across the boundaries.

- The intelligence community needs to have access, under safeguards, to a range of data to allow previously unexploitable sources of information to generate pre-emptive intelligence.
- The need for secure communications across the community and with the customers creates common priorities for the community as a whole to tackle.
- In the intelligence world, as in defence, governments are stewards of national capability, and strong central direction is needed to ensure that capabilities are built and maintained for the future.

All these factors point towards the need to continue to develop the UK intelligence community, going beyond the three Secret Agencies to include the central assessment staffs in the Cabinet Office, and the Joint Terrorism Analysis Centre and the Defence Intelligence Staff, respecting their position as an integral part of defence capability.

Some of the main lines of development are clear. The community has long had a central forum, the Joint Intelligence Community, and it now has a single head, at Permanent Secretary level, concerned both with the meaning of the intelligence provided for the Government, and thus its quality, and with the long-term health of the intelligence community. The Co-ordinator is already supported by a small planning, resources and programmes central staff, drawn largely from the Community itself, in order to formulate the long-term strategy for the Community and the annual statement of requirements for secret intelligence approved by the Ministerial Committee on Intelligence chaired by the Prime Minister. Cabinet Office staff support him in negotiating the Single Intelligence Account with the Chief Secretary to the Treasury, and in assessing the effectiveness of the community in meeting the requirements of its customers. What needs to be done here seems reasonably clear, as planning becomes more sophisticated and the agencies' own performance-management systems evolve. There are many parallels with the development of planning in MOD.

There are also lessons of what not to do that can be learned from the MOD experience. In creating a single Ministry of Defence in 1964, the pre-existing small Central Staff and Secretariat housed in Storey's Gate was bolted together with the three large traditional single-Service ministries. Over the subsequent years the centre of the new MOD expanded greatly to compensate, including adding a common procurement function for all three Services. The result was tensions and overlap. Now the centre is slimmed down and the overlap has been removed through creating genuine joint staffs, but it has been a long journey. In the intelligence world there is also central staff capacity that needs to be built up, not least to deliver compatible IT. But the principle of subsidiarity must reign, and the centre must be kept small. In that way the advantages of this evolution can be obtained without cutting across the statutory personal operational responsibilities of the Agency heads, and the general accountability to Parliament of their Secretaries of State. The Co-ordinator is, like the Cabinet Secretary, a servant of government as a whole.

Another key lesson from the defence experience is the value of retaining separate Armed Services while at the same time developing joint and combined operational capacity. I do not see the likely evolution in intelligence organization ending up with an agency merger. Collection of intelligence is a highly specialized activity that involves being able to recruit, train and motivate very different and unique kinds of people, even though (as the Armed Forces do in defence) the different specializations work closely together on individual operations. Although from time to time cost-cutters cast glances at the overheads of running three agencies, much has already been done to share the costs of genuinely common support. The loss of effectiveness of the diversion of emotional effort into new institution-building would be catastrophic at a time when all energies should be concentrated on the intelligence task. So the process that is under way, and that needs to be accelerated, is the combining of strong central strategic direction and planning, joint support and logistic functions, information systems, and so on, but retaining the agencies as the basic unit of organization and preserving their tradition of highly devolved operational management.

Let me cite one example of how this evolutionary process can successfully be accelerated. We know that the protective security and counter-terrorist customers want value-adding material brought together by subject, with the assurance that if there is any relevant material anywhere in the databases of the entire intelligence community then that will have been considered. That was the thinking behind the creation in 2003 of the Joint Terrorism Analysis Centre, which has become the UK's centre of expertise on international terrorism. JTAC exists to analyse and assess all types of intelligence relating to international terrorism, at home and overseas, to set threat levels and issue when necessary urgent warnings of likely terrorist activity, as well as producing detailed assessments of threats and other terrorist-related subjects for customers from a wide range of Government departments and agencies. It breaks new ground in being a self-standing organization comprised of representatives from 11 Government departments and agencies, including the police service, working within a circle of trust. The Head of JTAC is responsible to the Director General of the Security Service, who in turn reports to the Government's Joint Intelligence Committee on JTAC's activities. An Oversight Board, chaired by the Cabinet Office, checks that the requirements of the different customers for JTAC's work are actually being met.

I am conscious that other countries are also adapting their agencies and security forces to confront international terrorism and crime. There is no 'right' organizational model for intelligence and law enforcement that will fit all nations with their different traditions and legal systems. But there may be general principles that are common. Let me end this chapter with some reflections on the ideal arrangements that we might expect to find in any nation that was effectively dealing with the threat from jihadist terrorism. Such arrangements would, I submit, have at their heart concentric circles of trust:

- In an inner protected circle we should find a community of trust between the intelligence and security agencies, whether working on internal security or providing a service of human signals intelligence. Whatever national organizational geometry, there would be no legal barriers to co-operation in this circle. To borrow a phrase from Senator Pat Roberts, Chair of the US Senate Intelligence Committee, the watchword would be intelligence-sharing rather than compartmented intelligence access. There would be the trust necessary to make joint operations commonplace, spanning, where necessary, domestic and overseas. And you would see young officers training together, and taking part in cross-postings, really understanding what their colleagues from other disciplines may be able to bring to the party.
- Backed by appropriate legislation, the public would trust the intelligence community within that inner circle to use the most modern and effective techniques for acquiring and analysing the mass of communication, travel, border and other data needed to deal with terrorism and organized crime. There would be effective arrangement for parliamentary and judicial oversight, whose form would obviously depend upon national constitutions, but be

sufficient to provide public confidence that the use of these intrusive powers and the ability to share such information with overseas partners was properly regulated and proportionate.

- Widening to the next circle, we would see that secret intelligence community working hand in glove with the relevant police services, drawing on the latter's knowledge of the communities they serve. We would find secure arrangements for sharing operational detail within a circle of trust between those selected and vetted to work with the intelligence authorities on these sensitive operations. It would be for the police to use their independent authority to enforce the law, drawing on their close relationship with the community they serve, but targeted carefully by the secret work of the intelligence community using their most advanced methods. In this way the power of modern intelligence is harnessed for public protection, but without raising again in Europe the spectre of the secret policeman with their own legal authorities and the misuse of state power to collect personal information.

- And in a third circle of trust, the intelligence and police communities would belong to Government structures that enable them to share information and co-operate closely with the key staff in the Armed Forces and Defence Ministry, in the Foreign Ministry, and in Interior, Transport, Health, Environment and all those civil departments and local government engaged in 'homeland security' to provide the support for policy-making and overseas operations and assistance programmes, and to guide investment in improving national resilience.

- Finally, we would find that these circles had strong connections outside government, reaching out to the private sector who now run most of the critical national infrastructure that keeps modern life going.

- To recap briefly on my earlier argument, we would see these circles of trust form the secure national base on which sound international arrangements can be developed. Strategic assessments can be shared to guide the formation of collective security strategy and international agreements, timely operational warnings and terrorist assessments can be shared for public protection through the JTAC model, and not least the tactical pursuit of terrorist networks improved through bilateral relationships between the secret intelligence services of like-minded nations working together on specific operations and campaigns.

I do not want it to sound easier than it is. Intelligence structures, processes, co-ordination mechanisms that may have worked for nations in the past have to be rethought against the new threat and how it might develop. That is what the UK has had to do. It can involve changes that break with traditions. It will cost more money. But the status quo will no longer do.

6

Just Intelligence: Prolegomena to an Ethical Theory

Michael Quinlan

At various points in a career as a British civil servant, working mostly in the defence field, I was a customer of secret intelligence, and after leaving full-time government employment I carried out in 1994, for the Prime Minister of the day, a study on certain aspects of it. (Though the fact of this study soon became public knowledge, it was not until 2006 that limited elements of the report were released to public inspection at the National Archives.) I had long taken an interest in the ethics of military conflict, and in 2000, at an Oxford conference on intelligence (later reflected in a book)[1] I ventured the suggestion that there was a case for developing a theory of 'just intelligence', on the analogy of 'just-war' theory. I was subsequently challenged to contribute to such a task; and the present essay – by someone who is neither an intelligence professional nor a moral philosopher – offers accordingly some *prolegomena*, in the hope of providing stimulus to more thorough and expert addressal by others. In the course of developing it I have become increasingly aware that the field is very far from being untilled; but there is work yet to be done, particularly in the climate of heightened concern about intelligence work in the context of the 2003 invasion of Iraq.

1 Harold Shukman (ed.), *Agents for Change* (London: St Ermin's Press, 2000), pp. 61–71.

Two basic questions present themselves at the outset of reflection. First: why should we be concerned at all with ethics in this field? Is it not quintessentially one where Machiavelli and realpolitik have to rule? There are aspects of the intelligence business, as practised by all major countries, that seem notably disreputable by the behavioural standards of normal human settings; what purchase can ethics expect to have? '"Intelligence ethics" is an oxymoron', a long-serving officer from the US Central Intelligence Agency was once quoted as saying.[2] In the discussion at the Oxford conference one hardened intelligence professional – not from Britain or the United States – said of ethics in this field, with a dismissive wave of the hand, 'I leave all that to the clerics.' But that surely will not do. By contrast, Admiral Stansfield Turner, as Head of the US Central Intelligence Agency in the 1980s, said, 'There is one overall test of the ethics of human intelligence activities. That is whether those approving them feel they could defend their actions before the public if the actions became public.'[3] That is closer to the mark, if somewhat subjective. The fact is that inescapably and inherently (to adapt Aristotle) the human being is an ethical animal – that is part of what it means to be human. We can no more step outside ethics than we can opt out of the force of gravity. There is no area of human activity, whether public or private, collective or individual, that has an *a priori* entitlement to require the moralist to be silent. If the effective practice of intelligence raises awkward ethical questions, we are obliged ultimately to face them.

A consideration at a less elevated level, from practical expediency, points in the same direction. In most major Western countries over the last couple of decades, and especially since

---

2   Duane R. Clarridge, quoted in *New York Times*, 2 February 2006.
3   Stansfield Turner, *Security and Democracy* (London: Sedgwick & Jackson, 1986).

the 2003 Iraq episode, the business of intelligence has for a
mix of reasons emerged from the shadows into open view far
more fully than was customary in the past, notably in the
United Kingdom. Our publics, thus increasingly aware of the
activity, would not long remain content that what is undertaken in their name should be exempt from moral standard,
constraint and scrutiny.

The second basic question comes at the matter from a different angle: why should intelligence need any distinctive
ethical consideration, any more than do other governmental
activities like diplomacy, bureaucratic administration or
military procurement? The answer lies in the characteristic
already noted: that its effective practice seems unavoidably
to entail doing some things that are plainly and seriously
contrary to the moral rules accepted as governing most human
activity.

The just-war paradigm

The 'Stansfield Turner' criterion, taken in isolation, lacks
objective anchorage. We must look for something more systematic. In the search for that, the paradigm of the just-war
tradition[4] suggests a starting-point. The thinkers who developed that tradition were wrestling with the harsh tension
between two truths about the activity of war, both of which
seemed inescapable. The first was that it entailed doing things
– above all, killing people – which in any ordinary context
were gravely wrong. The second was that amid the bitter
realities of human existence it surely did not make practical
sense – and therefore not moral sense – to demand that the
entire activity of war be dismissed by pacifist anathema

---

4   For a brief overview see Michael Quinlan, 'Justifying War' in *Australian
Journal of International Affairs*, Vol. 58, No. 1, March 2004, pp. 7–15.

insisting that the virtuous abstain from it. What emerged from the wrestling was the concept, elaborated over many centuries, of two levels of moral discipline to govern and limit the activity of war, within the broader context of the duty of public authorities for sustaining the well-being of their people – a goal that remains in itself, especially in relation to tolerably well-ordered polities, a proper ethical good; national interest (to use a modern term) is not an amoral concept. One level of discipline concerned the criteria that ought to be met if war was to be justly undertaken – *jus ad bellum*. The other concerned the constraints and prohibitions that ought to be observed in the conduct of war once entered into – *jus in bello*.

It is unnecessary here to go into the detailed content of either set of criteria. The point for the present analysis is that this seems a natural way to approach the ethical analysis of any activity that poses, *prima facie*, considerations in awkward tension, through purporting to require or allow conduct towards others that would be reprehensible in most ordinary situations. The rest of this chapter seeks to explore how far and in what ways the activity of intelligence as practised by the state (issues about information-gathering by the media or other commercial organizations are not addressed here) has to be viewed as presenting major ethical considerations in apparent opposition to one another; and what we might begin to say about the conditions under which it may properly be engaged in – *jus ad intelligentiam*, as it were – and about the limitations that ought to be observed in carrying it out even when it is properly undertaken – *jus in intelligentia*.

Two general difficulties about examining the subject need to be acknowledged. First, far less is dependably known about what is really done in the business of intelligence than in the business of war. There are mountains of vivid fiction, a certain amount of shrewd conjecture and hint, and some wary memoir-writing, but the vast majority of citizens do not know and cannot readily find out in any specific, comprehensive and dependable way precisely what intelligence professionals do in concrete day-to-day operational terms, in the way and degree that we know or can find out what it is that soldiers do. Notably authentic glimpses of some aspects were provided in 2004 and 2005 through after-the-event inquiries in the United States and the United Kingdom into the role played by intelligence in relation to the 2003 Iraq war. The report of the Committee of Privy Counsellors chaired by Lord Butler of Brockwell[5] is a vivid British example. But these were special and limited instances.

The second general difficulty is partly related to the first. There might be real disadvantage – not just presentational discomfort – in having governments make to potential adversaries and wrong-doers a public present of extensive and detailed knowledge about exactly what public authorities will and will not be prepared to do in gathering information. There is again a partial analogy here with the use of military force – consider, for example, the matter of nuclear-weapon targeting for deterrence, on which governments have scarcely ever been willing to go beyond making, at most, very general statements rather than spell out exact limits to the action they would regard as tolerable *in extremis*. And the underlying consideration seems, if anything, even more cogent in respect of intelligence than of war.

All that noted, we can with reasonable confidence say a number of descriptive things about intelligence work. First, much of it consists simply of carefully collating and analysing material that is available to anyone with the resources and inclination to gather it, especially in the modern world of

5   *Review of Intelligence on Weapons of Mass Destruction: Report of a Committee of Privy Counsellors* (London: Stationery Office, HC 808, 14 July 2004).

enormous information flows. No moral problem arises there. Second, within the category of intelligence information that is not available more or less openly, a great deal is collected by eavesdropping of one sort or another – picking up communications not meant to be heard by outsiders, breaking codes that are intended to conceal content, and the like, including also watching activities which the actor would have preferred to keep unobserved. It is not obvious that this is in itself seriously wrong in moral terms; in ordinary life it may often be a breach of courtesy or social convention, but scarcely a grave evil. It may in some circumstances be imprudent to eavesdrop – for example, while it might be highly interesting to install listening devices in the offices of high functionaries of friendly countries, the penalties of being found doing so might well greatly outweigh the advantages of knowing whatever might be learned. But that is essentially a calculation about expediency, not moral value. Eavesdropping by intelligence may nevertheless sometimes entail breaking the law, if not of the eavesdropper's country then at least of the target country, and perhaps international law, as in Cold War penetration of territorial waters or airspace by intelligence-gathering vehicles; and infringement of law is in itself *prima facie* in need of special justification.

In addition, at least some eavesdropping is in itself, and almost irrespective of the method employed, constrained by particular agreements voluntarily entered into between states; and it may be that it would be in the general interest to widen the ambit of such agreements.[6] Whether or not there is such a widening, any deliberate breach of such commitments must import moral as well as prudential considerations; but it is

---

6   See the discussion by Michael Herman in L. V. Scott and Peter Jackson (eds), *Understanding Intelligence in the Twenty-First Century* (London: Routledge, 2004), pp. 187–92.

then primarily the fact of breaching agreement rather than the inherent nature of eavesdropping that would raise the moral considerations.

But third, it can be no secret that some of what is done in intelligence-gathering, above all in the category commonly known as HUMINT ('human intelligence') entails a good deal more than eavesdropping. This chapter does not address what is commonly called 'covert action' in the sense of physical intervention to disrupt or prevent, not merely to discover, what an adversary does; that raises other considerations. Even short of that, however, HUMINT and other comparable intelligence business have to involve, just for example, readiness to tell untruths about who and what one is. Conventional fictions such as the Ruritanian Embassy presenting as its Deputy Assistant Cultural Attaché a tough-looking personage of no obvious aesthetic sensibility present no problem, but covert operators have to be prepared to tell untruths seriously intended to mislead public officials like immigration officers or policemen who customarily have a particular right to be told the truth. Another example might be stealing the documents of another government; and a further and harsher one might be turning a blind eye at least temporarily to serious crimes being committed – perhaps even, still more disquietingly, standing by when one could have prevented them – individuals with whom one is interacting, in order to remain deceptively in their confidence for larger purposes like penetrating a murderous terrorist organization. (A partial parallel is the occasional acceptance by British authorities in World War II, so it is understood, of losses or reverses which the knowledge gleaned by the 'ULTRA' code-breaking success could have been exploited to prevent, but only at the cost of forfeiting greater long-term benefits expected from continuing to conceal from the enemy that his signals traffic was being read.) A yet further instance is that of inducing individuals in other countries to breach the formal duties and loyalties of their public functions or their citizenship, and thereafter protecting them in that breaching. Professional insiders could undoubtedly construct a longer catalogue, but the examples noted above suffice for the present analysis.

This evident reality, of doing things that in normal settings would merit condemnation, is one component of the moral tension that besets the activity of intelligence; it is the analogue, in the just-war comparison, of the fact that engaging in war entails readiness to kill. In the just-war context the other component of the tension is that it seems repugnant to practical and therefore to moral common sense to hold that one must therefore never engage in war even to stop an Attila or a Hitler. The analogue of this in the intelligence context would need to assert that it is similarly repugnant to practical and moral common sense to hold that we must never engage in intelligence activity of the kinds just exemplified, even to thwart murderous terrorists or to strengthen our ability to resist wicked aggression. Governments throughout the world have plainly been prepared to make that assertion. The next stage in analysis is to consider what reasons might warrant it.

We need not attempt a comprehensive inventory – which might be long[7] – of situations or objectives in regard to which it would be unreasonable to dismiss clandestine intelligence-gathering as immoral, or as conferring too little distinctive benefit to warrant accepting ethical drawbacks. (The adjective 'clandestine' is hereafter used as shorthand for intelligence collection that has recourse to methods breaching normal ethical rules. Some of what has been described above as eaves-dropping and judged to be in itself morally unproblematic is also clandestine in the normal sense of the word, but that is

---

7   For a preliminary survey see *Agents for Change, op. cit.*, pp. 62–5.

not what will be referred to.) Two categories provide illustration. The first concerns terrorism. It would be absurd to disqualify wholesale the use of mendacious deception to penetrate sinister organizations like al-Qaeda now, or in Northern Ireland's past the Provisional Irish Republican Army or its 'Loyalist' counterparts, so as to enhance the chances of preventing lethal violence. It by no means follows that absolutely anything goes in achieving and sustaining such penetration, but wholesale prohibition cannot be right. The other illustration is espionage against enemies in time of war, as by the United Kingdom against Nazi Germany. That needs no explanatory comment.

The foregoing paragraphs sketch a framework similar to that underlying just-war reasoning. They portray an activity which at least in some respects cannot be conducted effectively without cutting across normal moral expectations, but which is essential for public purposes that seem plainly of compelling moral necessity and rightness. In just-war analysis, however, that does not mean that we can morally engage in any war we like, and then fight it in any way we like; any exemptions from 'normal' ethical behaviour have to be justified and limited. Similarly, we cannot engage in the particular class of intelligence activity here labelled 'clandestine' against any target we like, or use any methods we like.

Invoking the concept of 'moral common sense' does not presuppose a purely utilitarian or consequentialist philosophy of public ethics. The just-war tradition does not contend that, in war, good aims and expectations of good eventual outcomes justify any means. In accepting that there is an entitlement if necessary to kill enemy soldiers, it holds that by the nature of their role such soldiers forfeit the normal human right not to be killed; and at the same time it typically recognizes some deontological imperatives – that is, that there are some things that absolutely ought not to be done even to facilitate victory over an appalling aggressor. The application of the paradigm to 'just intelligence' must be ready to acknowledge comparable dimensions both of entitlement and of constraint. Entitlement might rest, in the broadest terms, on a concept that we may legitimately collect information, even – perhaps especially? – in the face of attempts to withhold it, about activities that might lead to unjust injury to those for whom we have responsibility. Constraint would accept that there are some methods of collection that must never be used, however severe we may judge the possible injury to be, and some that must not be used disproportionately – that is, in circumstances where the breach of normal moral rules is more severe than the importance of the legitimate objective reasonably warrants.

Against that background, issues arise about what sorts of limit might be appropriate in the selection of targets for clandestine intelligence-gathering – *jus ad intelligentiam* – and then in the choice of methods for such gathering – *jus in intelligentia*.

Jus ad intelligentiam

There is a very broad potential spectrum of things about which governments would like to get knowledge through their intelligence services, in the widest sense of finding out or confirming things which it would be helpful to them to know but which the targets – whether states or other entities – are either unwilling or unable to disclose promptly and dependably, and which cannot be discovered as promptly and dependably, or perhaps at all, by other means. At one extreme of the spectrum there might be getting solid warning of terrorist plans to blow up Parliament; at the other, finding out what is the 'bottom line' of the Ruritanian Government in an impending negotiation about tariffs on trade in cabbages. Clandestine intelligence-gathering would clearly be justified on the former; but it seems hard, as a matter of proportionate judgement, to maintain that it would be so on the latter. I consider later a subsidiary issue about whether the moral situation is altered if we have grounds for believing that the Ruritanians are themselves engaged in clandestine intelligence-gathering about our own 'bottom line'. That particular point aside, however, the question is where along the spectrum the line of prohibition or limitation ought to be drawn. For added complication, is it a single line or a series of lines, with a considerable array of clandestine methods morally allowable at the top end of the threat spectrum – that is, the end exemplified by major terrorism – but perhaps only a more modest and restricted set at intermediate points? Many subject-matters may lie between the extremes. The development of military capability by states whose long-term peaceful intentions towards us or our friends we believe we cannot take wholly on trust? The faithful observance of arms control agreements like the 1968 Nuclear Non-Proliferation Treaty or the 1972 Biological Weapons Convention, or of mandatory United Nations Security Council resolutions? Savage internal repression by tyrannical regimes? Narcotics traffic? International organized crime of other sorts? Illegal immigration networks? Violent animal-rights protest? Large-scale and deliberate breach of agreed rules on trade?

It is surely evident that dividing lines ought to be drawn somewhere along the spectrum of iniquity to be countered and proper interest to be served; but it is much harder to formulate clear and precise proposals for where or how to draw them. A first approximation might suggest that we are entitled to use clandestine means (still in the special sense of 'clandestine' explained earlier) if other means do not seem likely to suffice – that remains an important qualification, analogous to the just-war criterion of 'last resort' – in order to collect information that we reasonably believe may help us to forestall, counter or alleviate actions that would be seriously damaging to peaceful and constitutional order, or to the lives or the major human rights of our own people or of others towards whom we accept significant responsibilities.

There is a great deal packed into that first approximation; and the application of some of its elements would be highly judgemental – just how damaging is 'seriously damaging', for example? Al-Qaeda's plans, yes; those Ruritanian cabbages, surely no; but what about action that could inflict grave economic damage leading to real hardship to our citizens, like attempts to disrupt flows or distort prices in the international oil market? The economic field cannot be totally excluded. It is inescapable that any general principle, however skilfully shaped, will always leave a large middle ground within which there have to be judgements made in all the particular circumstances, with ample room accordingly for disagreement and dispute, whether in good faith or in bad, about on which side of the permissibility boundary particular intelligence targets fall. That is in the nature of practical affairs amid the manifold complexities of human life. Similar judgemental uncertainties often beset the application of just-war concepts; but those concepts, honestly applied, can nevertheless often lead to clear and important conclusions. That can be equally true of just intelligence.

Jus in intelligentia

If clandestine intelligence-gathering is to be conducted effectively, actions like (for example) agent-runners telling untruths about who they are or what they are doing are unavoidable. It seems unavoidable also that they will have to be ready to exploit the willingness of individuals from the target country, or in whatever else is the target field, to act in breach of normal loyalties. But are there limits to what they should be prepared to do in order to generate or exploit that willingness?

Ideological persuasion? Bribery, in one form or another? So far, perhaps reasonable. But blackmail? Fostering narcotics addiction? Entrapment? Threat to family? Surely not.

Once more, no ready formula suggests itself for where the line should be drawn between the permissible and the impermissible, especially since, as implied earlier, it might be appropriate to draw the line in different places according to the gravity, and perhaps also the imminence and probability, of the harm we are seeking to forestall or diminish. Such a concept would be the analogue of the just-war criterion of proportionality. Broadly, however, the line of prohibition might relate to whether serious coercive violence – or its near-equivalent, as in blackmail – is done to individuals whom we are not entitled to harm. The point of that last qualification – 'whom we are not entitled to harm' – is that in, for example, World War II it would surely have been legitimate to kill an enemy sentry in the course of a breaking-and-entering operation to get crucial operational information. That would be a justifiable warlike action; but it would scarcely be allowable in peacetime, though circumstances approaching those of wartime might arise over imminent terrorism.

There then arises the difficult matter of interrogation, which is often an aspect of intelligence-gathering and has been the focus of especial public debate and concern in recent years. What is legitimate? Arbitrary and sometimes covert imprisonment, as in Guantanamo Bay? – not of that scale and duration, many (including this writer) would say. More awkward still, what is to be said about torture, and what exactly is to be classified as that? Little respect worldwide has been accorded to, or merited by, attempts made within the Administration of President George W. Bush to redefine 'torture' away from its natural meaning and from the definition in the 1984 UN Convention Against Torture, to which the United States is a party, so as to encompass only extreme actions at the top end of the term's range as normally understood. It is at least more honest to claim, as others in that Administration or supporting it have occasionally done, that torture may be justified (subject perhaps to some procedural safeguards) if the end is pressing and important enough. But though it is possible to imagine elaborate and far-out scenarios in which the temptation might seem very cogent, that claim ought to be firmly rejected for reasons both of ultimate moral principle and of pragmatism (including the grave 'slippery-slope' danger). Even within a more moderate ethical calculus, however, and quite aside from considerations about the frequent unreliability of information gained under torture and also about the damage which use of such methods entails to any prospect of subsequent criminal prosecution, there are questions of definition, as was seen in the 1970s when the British Government changed its practices to conform with the finding of the European Court of Human Rights against some of the methods which had occasionally been used in the counter-terrorist campaign in Northern Ireland. It would be absurd to say that interrogation, perhaps of people whose malignity is incontestable, must be conducted entirely without pressure – in a comfortable armchair, as it were, with a cup of tea and a biscuit every hour and no harsh expression or frightening tone. Again, some general guideline is needed to anchor judgement. The core of the formulation in the 1984 Convention (tighter than United States domestic law appears to be) seems well framed for the purpose – 'the intentional infliction of severe physical or mental pain or suffering to obtain information or a confession'.

There is, however, a yet further issue in this zone: the matter of what might be called 'torture at second hand'. Media accounts have exposed a practice termed 'extraordinary rendition', meaning handing over terrorist suspects to friendly countries whom there is reason to think less scrupulous than the hander-over about the methods of interrogation used. That would seem plainly wrong as a deliberate action, and it is indeed prohibited by the 1984 Convention. But another awkward question arises: even where the handover of individuals is not in question, what should be the moral evaluation of continuing intelligence co-operation and information exchange – for example, over international terrorism, with countries known to use methods which we ourselves regard as wrongful? If we come into possession of particular information that is operationally important for the protection of our people, we cannot expunge it from our minds or artificially pretend not to know it even if we believe or suspect it to have been wrongfully acquired; but a systematic and ongoing relationship – to sustain which, moreover, we may be expected to divulge information about individuals as well as to receive it – is a different matter. It is not easy to find a ready answer to this problem, which is the more awkward in that it may sometimes in practice be precisely from countries where the risk of brutal interrogation may be high that information about terrorism is most needed.

There is some similarity here with the problem noted earlier, of how we are to justify continuing to work, in our penetration of terrorist or other criminal organizations, with individuals whom we know to be engaged in evildoing. Once more, any purist demand for perfectly clean hands, both directly and at one remove or more, is not easy to square with practical realities – realities, moreover, which are becoming increasingly the normal context of intelligence work, as the prime working environment shifts away from classical inter-state conflict.

We might consider now the 'Everybody does it' argument – the right of retaliation, from another standpoint. If we have reason to believe that others are collecting intelligence against us for purposes or by methods which we ourselves would prefer to rule out, are we thereby dispensed from our own obligations? The simple answer to this is 'No', or at least 'Not entirely'. If the obligations are founded not on basic moral principle but on particular agreement or received international law, then indeed serious breach of the bargain by other parties may properly remove or diminish their entitlement to remain protected by the agreement or law. To take again an analogy from the context of war, it is likely that some limited use of chemical weapons would not always or in all circumstances have been contrary to moral principle on the discriminate and proportionate use of military force, but under the 1925 Geneva Protocol, states agreed to abstain from it entirely. Many of them, however, attached a rider to the effect that if an adversary breached the Protocol, the right to retaliate was reserved. That was justifiable; but there would still, in any such use, have been a moral duty to continue to abide by the more basic ethical constraints – not to retaliate against non-combatants or with a severity disproportionate to proper military objectives, whatever the adversary might have done. Similarly, if there is an agreement with the authorities of Country X that we will not collect intelligence covertly from one another, but we then find that Country X is in fact doing so, we would be entitled in retaliation to eavesdrop (rather as during the Cold War there seems to have been almost a tacit agreement, one or two special episodes apart, not to make much public fuss about the intrusive intelligence-gathering operations which both sides conducted in breach of strict international law). But we would not be entitled to extract information by entrapment, blackmail or torture, even if Country X is guilty of such methods.

The discussion so far has operated within the broad structural paradigm of just-war reasoning. In at least one respect, however, intelligence calls for a wider paradigm. Beyond the activity of collecting intelligence there lies that of using it, and distinctive ethical questions can arise there too. This is not a matter only of whether the intelligence product is culpably distorted (whether by provider or recipient) to fit policy preference, or its limitations and uncertainties brushed aside in order to justify or at least not impede decisions desired on other grounds – issues such as those which the Butler Committee and its counterpart in the United States examined over the 2003 invasion of Iraq. Most of the moral questions in this area are general ones bearing upon any use of evidence, not peculiar to that collected by secret intelligence effort. But where, as is usually the case with secret intelligence, the evidence is for good reason not made available openly for all hearers to probe and test, a special moral responsibility lies upon intelligence authorities and their customers not to claim wider knowledge or greater certainty than is genuinely warranted – not to assert, for example, that evidence is 'extensive, detailed and authoritative'[8] when its true quality is such that objective evaluation of the same evidence by a broadly composed committee of inquiry can lead its chairman to conclude that it is in reality 'very thin'.[9]

There are moral issues also about the use of secret intelligence when it is brought to bear in ways that touch seriously upon the rights of individuals. It would normally be wrong for public authorities to use to the disadvantage of individuals information which those individuals had no opportunity to test or rebut, and of which they might even be wholly unaware. Yet the product of intelligence is occasionally used in such ways – for example, to trigger intrusion into normal privacy, to refuse or limit public employment through processes like vetting, or more recently and controversially in decisions to restrict liberty or withdraw right of residence. Moreover, such actions by government may often rest upon

8   British Prime Minister Tony Blair on Iraqi possession of weapons of mass destruction (House of Commons Official Report, column 3, 24 September 2002).
9   Lord Butler of Brockwell (House of Lords Official Report, column 463, 7 September 2004) .

judgements of probability, not upon proof of the standard that court proceedings in criminal justice customarily require. Given the entitlement of our societies to be protected so far as possible from grave risks, we cannot reasonably say that the product of intelligence must absolutely never be so used where we perceive pressing danger from traitors or terrorists, or as it was during the Cold War when Western countries honestly believed that this was necessary in order to guard against grave potential threat from the Soviet Union. Once more there is no escape from having to weigh conflicting considerations, rather than resting on some neat and comprehensive rule. The weighing must, however, have an ethical dimension and take into account, alongside whatever are the proper benefits that we believe can be secured in no other way, the limitations and uncertainties of secret intelligence, as well as the disagreeable (and ultimately even corrupting) subtractions which its use in such circumstances entails from the customary and proper standards of open democratic societies, and in the long term from the valuable wider respect in which such societies seek to be held. The bar ought to be set high.

Conclusion

There are further aspects of the topic on which this chapter has not attempted to touch, such as the proper relationship of intelligence activity with one's own domestic law. (Should the duty of obedience to that law be regarded as absolute, or as open to be qualified in extreme circumstances by considerations of proportionality?) In brief, however, secret intelligence-gathering is a valuable, sometimes even an indispensable, tool in the ability of public authorities to fulfil their duties of protection towards those for whose well-being they bear responsibility. Its effective conduct must sometimes require that action be taken which ought in most contexts to be regarded as morally wrong.

In face of that tension we cannot say that morality must simply be set aside; we have to identify some conceptual structure for legitimating and disciplining the activity. An ethical framework is needed in at least two parts: the first for delineating the purposes important enough to justify some stepping outside normal ethical expectation, and the second to limit how far that stepping outside may reach and what forms it may take.

It would be absurd and offensive to suggest that intelligence professionals in countries like those of the West do not already have ethical concepts which they bring to bear on what they do. For reasons sketched earlier, it would moreover be unrealistic to expect to frame an open and explicit code in specific terms to govern the entire activity. There would, however, be merit – not least for public confidence and support – in seeking to develop a wider and more systematic understanding of principles than seems yet to have been generally established and recognized on either side of the Atlantic.

7

The Dilemmas of Using Secret Intelligence for Public Security[1]

David Omand

Those designing the security apparatus of the Cold War, the 'Secret State' as Peter Hennessy has so ably chronicled it, had their share of dilemmas to resolve over ensuring public security. The protection of the public from the military threat from Soviet Communism rested not on civil defence but on nuclear deterrence, preventing the Soviet Union from being able to use the threat of its massive military forces to coerce Western Europe. That defensive strategy depended crucially on convincing Soviet planners of their inability to achieve strategic surprise that would have left the Western nuclear powers with no other choice than admit defeat or resort to suicidal escalation. Soviet planners had therefore to be brought to believe that the British Government had thought through all the implications of their strategy of deterrence. Such preparations had to show that the UK was fully prepared to be able to draw on the full range of its nuclear options if need be to preserve national independence, while being seen to have

---

1   A full account of the case for the ethical code described here can be found in Sir D. Omand, 'Ethical Guidelines in Using Secret Intelligence for Public Security', *The Cambridge Review of International Affairs*, Vol. 19, No. 4 (2006). Earlier versions of this material were delivered at the Royal Institute for International Affairs, King's College, London, the Cambridge University Centre for International Studies, and St Antony's College, Oxford.

reassured the British public that they were safer that way despite the horror of the contemplation of relying on nuclear deterrence. The Soviet planners had, for example, to be convinced that the UK had made provision for maintaining the continuity of government and thus the flexibility of response in even the most extreme of circumstances.

At the same time it was crucial to the working of deterrence that the potential opponent should not learn the detail of these arrangements, other than knowing that they existed, were obviously thorough and were well tested. It was a logical consequence therefore that the British public also had to be kept in the dark about the full extent of what was being done in their name, literally as well as figuratively under the surface. Only recently has the public been able to learn, for example, of the full extent of the network of regional headquarters with the huge underground site prepared for central government in the event of nuclear war, and to learn generally of the hidden wiring of the Cold War secret state.

It was on these sombre matters that I reflected when preparing a speech I was due to give at the launch of The Secret State Exhibition at the National Archives in 2004. I felt a distinct kinship with the then (1946–62) Cabinet Secretary Norman Brook and his Cold War planners in my own work as UK Security and Intelligence Co-ordinator designing the architecture for national resilience and public security against the threats and risks of the twenty-first century, not least from international terrorism. What we had principally in common was the need to envisage the unthinkable, however disturbing. Of course the weight of our effort had to be on devising strategies to prevent it from happening, but also to prepare for what we would do to mitigate the impact if the worst should happen. The term 'resilience', a borrowing from the science of materials, came into use to describe our vision of a society that would be able to absorb sudden shocks and yet bounce back quickly into its normal shape.

There was one clear difference from the disaster planning of the past: the strategy we were to follow and the framework within which national protection would be built, such as the complete recasting of emergency legislation (the Civil Contingencies Act 2004), could not – and should not – be kept secret. Our work had to be explained to the public whose active support and participation would be essential, both directly and through partnerships with local government, businesses and community and voluntary organizations. In coining in my speech the term 'the protecting state' (or 'the protective state', as it has become in the title of this book) I wanted to mark that break with the past. The primary duty of government is still public protection, but in a world of multiple threats and risks the public have to be trusted to be players.

Some of the dilemmas we thus faced in the recasting of strategy for twenty-first-century public protection had an eery resonance with those faced by the Cold War planners. In relation to terrorism today, for example, with only limited resources available, who or what should be given priority for protection? Should we concentrate on what the Cold War game theorists would call a 'minimax' strategy, of minimizing the maximum damage that might be done to the life of the nation; and thus ensure the protection of the essentials of life, or, as the jargon has it, the critical national infrastructure (government, power, communications, etc.) from the consequences of major attack? Or should we follow a modern version of a 'maximin' strategy, maximizing the minimum level of security that members of the public ought to enjoy in their everyday lives as they go to work, frequent public spaces or use air travel? The answer so far of course has had to be a judicious admixture of both approaches.

Some dilemmas over public education seem more acute today than in the Cold War past. Nowhere is that more the case than with the issues that arise because of the key role that intelligence plays in public protection against jihadist terrorism. The hottest part of the Cold War was the battle between the opposing intelligence services probing each other's defences, including the 'spy versus counter-spy' annals of the period. It is also the case that intelligence-derived knowledge, or what was judged at the time to be the best available approximation to such knowledge, of the nuclear weapons and other military capability and intentions of the Soviet Union and the Warsaw Pact, shaped policy. But apart from fuelling material for spy novels, knowledge of the vital role of intelligence was largely confined to the intelligence community and their 'pol-mil' (politico-military) customers. Only the periodic defection or security scandal and the exaggerations of the thriller writers brought these matters up to the surface.

Today the position could not be more different. Protection from jihadist terrorism is directly linked in the public mind to the effectiveness of our intelligence in uncovering and frustrating terrorist plots. Public interest is not just in testing the validity of the intelligence assessment behind policy responses such as the use of counter-terrorist or immigration legislation (as observed by the sceptical judgement of the Law Lord, Lord Hoffman,[2] 'The real threat to the life of the nation, in the sense of a people living in accordance with its traditional laws and political values, comes not from terrorism but from laws such as these. That is the true measure of what terrorism may achieve. It is for Parliament to decide whether to give the terrorists such a victory'). The adequacy of tactical intelligence itself has become a front-page issue – witness the calls for a public inquiry into intelligence behind the very visible Forest Gate

---

2   House of Lords, Session 2004–05_[2004] UKHL 56 Judgments – 'A (FC) and others (FC) (Appellants) v. Secretary of State for the Home Department (Respondent)'.

police raid (June 2006) that failed to net the expected suspects and their weapons. The calls to legislate to allow more secret intelligence to be used in securing convictions for terrorist offences in court also create a dilemma: bringing terrorists and their supporters to justice depends upon the deployment in court of highly sensitive material from secret sources such as human agents or electronic bugging. Due process has to be balanced by the need to protect intelligence sources, methods and effort. The real intelligence struggle with the terrorists must always be conducted in the shadows, but the dilemma of how much of it to reveal for the honest purposes of public safety and education and in the interests of justice remains.

We cannot escape the conclusion that achieving any acceptable level of public security from the current and expected threat of jihadist terrorism will continue to depend on having pre-emptive intelligence to uncover and disrupt terrorist networks at home and overseas. What is more, successful action to counter so-called 'domestic terrorism', the sources of jihadist violence within British Muslim communities, will come in large part from developing intelligence leads volunteered from within those communities themselves. There must therefore be widespread public confidence in the integrity and methods of the intelligence and security authorities, and confidence that individual rights will be protected.

Public tolerance of security measures (including tough counter-terrorism laws) comes from an understanding of the necessity for them that rests on an appreciation of the dangers that terrorism poses – and that in turn depends upon a belief in the integrity of the assessments of the threat that government and police make publicly available. The infamous Iraq WMD dossier showed how problematic it can be to try to recast intelligence assessments for a lay audience so that the public knows the background to the reasons why the Government has felt compelled to act. The handling of that dossier has also shown the risks of government appearing to use the professional reputation of their intelligence advisers to bolster their justification of their policies. Intelligence assessment and policy advocacy do not comfortably co-exist. Yet that is in essence the everyday dilemma facing the police, security authorities and ministers after every controversial counter-terrorist operation or new security measure or legislative proposal that has to be justified to a curious and possibly sceptical public.

Revolutionary jihadism represents a very hard target for the intelligence community to penetrate, since it is organized around tight cells of dedicated extremists with linkages that rely on kinship, personal relationships and recommendations built on shared experience such as attendance at al-Qaeda training camps. Past British experience – for example, in fighting Irish terrorism – has been that it is secret intelligence that provides the best clues and early indications that can lead to the uncovering of terrorist active service units and support networks. Armed with good pre-emptive intelligence, counter-terrorist operations can be designed and focused on legitimate targets without dislocating the normal life of the community and without creating a sense of discrimination in the application of security measures. And good intelligence informs the understanding of the reasons for the violence and thus guides the search for strategy that goes beyond combating the terrorists themselves.

One response to the situation across the world has been for governments to increase significantly the overall resources allocated to security and intelligence work. The UK is no exception. The British Security Service will, for example, soon be double the size it was before 9/11, a move that has considerable public support. Additionally, however, the pressure is on intelligence communities to generate more actionable intelligence from these resources by extending the range of methods judged acceptable in the pursuit of public safety, and to use the product more aggressively to strike more directly at the terrorists themselves. These pressures create real dilemmas for governments and for their intelligence agencies in defining what are acceptable boundaries of their conduct.

At the heart of many of these dilemmas in the use of intelligence for public protection is the need simultaneously to reassure the majority that sufficient is being done for their security to allow them (in the words of the British Government's strategic counter-terrorist objective) to go about their normal business freely and with confidence, while demonstrating, especially to Muslim communities, that government is acting in consonance with its own approach to human rights and justice. In the case of the UK in particular, is government following the logic of its own long-term counter-terrorist strategy with its emphasis on the need to prevent the radicalization of a fresh generation of young Muslims? Can the minority communities from whom the terrorists might hope to seek support be reassured that they are not being stigmatized or discriminated against domestically, at the same time as vigorous and effective intelligence-led action is taken to remove the existing terrorists from the community? This need for reassurance extends to being able to demonstrate that the methods being used by our partners in the wider fight against terrorism overseas are in keeping with the underlying values of a democratic state ruled by law. Such reassurance is additionally difficult to give, it must be added, when the Government itself is acutely sensitive about the part that the Iraq war now plays as a radicalizing influence.

Meeting even reasonable, and certainly managing unreasonable, public expectations for security is also hard for government when it is under the repeated hammer of populist feeling expressed through sections of the red-top media. There is, I suspect, much sensible recognition by members of the travelling public of the need to manage the risks involved in tackling terrorism in a measured way. There are helpful signs in the growing aversion to the extremes of a 'health and safety' culture that would distort much-valued aspects of normal life for the sake of marginal gains in safety. British stoicism in the face of real adversity is legendary. Nevertheless, given the publicity associated with such attacks as have taken place in the UK or overseas affecting British citizens, expectations of the level of protection that governments can offer are probably still unrealistically high. The intelligence community certainly knows all too well that, despite their many successes, when terrorists do get through under the security radar, the first accusation will be that this was because of a failure of intelligence. We know, however, from experience that intelligence coverage can never be expected to be complete, analysts are fallible and operational activity often involves an element of mistaken judgement or events not going according to plan. There will inevitably be further casualties in a long campaign.

One lesson hard-won from experience in previous campaigns that is worth recalling is that taking short cuts, and letting ends justify means, in the hope of quick knockout blows against the terrorists is self-defeating. One example can be found in the consequences of the use in 1971 by British authorities in Northern Ireland of internment coupled with 'deep interrogation' techniques. The result was very limited additional intelligence at the cost of a propaganda disaster that turned many moderates in the community against the authorities, particularly after the European Court of Human Rights found that the British methods amounted to brutal and degrading treatment.[3] Over the same period, heavy-handed security measures, such as house-to-house searches and undue

---

3   Ireland v. The United Kingdom, 5310/71 [1978] ECHR 1, 18 January 1978.

use of 'stop and search' powers, impacted on the innocent and ill-intentioned alike and thus became themselves radicalizing factors among those from whom the extremists hoped to recruit.

Most of the ethical problems associated with legislation to counter terrorism, including facilitating intelligence-gathering, thus centre on how one might arrive at the appropriate mix for the circumstances in question of individual categories of rights, such as the right to life with the right to be protected by the state from threats to oneself and one's family, and the right to privacy of personal and family life. There is an obvious danger that security concerns are somehow thought always to trump consideration of human rights with the desire for immediate security gain as having automatic primacy. It is a balancing act within rights that should be sought, and not a trade-off between rights and a separate public good called security.

It is also a balancing act to ensure that long-term domestic and international impact of the methods chosen for proposed intelligence and security operations is properly assessed, as well as the hoped-for immediate gains. Democratic governments will always be more comfortable applying utilitarian – greatest good for the greatest number – judgements in their balancing acts rather than appealing to higher ethical principles, and they will find it easier in so doing if they ensure that long-term strategic as well as tactical considerations are included – thus, for example, avoiding the obvious trap of desirable immediate security benefits for the majority justifying actions that will come to be seen as disproportionately affecting a minority.

Let me cite some examples to help illustrate the nature of some of the current dilemmas in the use and collection of secret intelligence.

We have seen, since 9/11, intelligence used to direct military force to strike overtly at known locations of terrorist activity overseas in order to disrupt terrorist planning, training and logistics pipelines and to disable terrorist leadership. Such NATO-led operations, for example, continue in support of the Government of Afghanistan. But in addition, as part of the so-called 'global war on terror', we have also seen the use, outside the battlefield, of intelligence to guide military or covert lethal action against terrorists. We have seen 'targeted killing' by US Forces, for example, by precision-guided air strike, presumably following determination by the US President that the individual terrorists concerned may be killed, if located, and if capture is not feasible.[4] The Israeli Government is currently defending before its Supreme Court its own policy of extra-judicial killing.[5] Such direct action might be deemed acceptable in a war zone against an identified combatant in accordance with the rules of war. But what legal framework can provide for use by military or covert forces of such pre-emptive lethal force outside the battlefield? Should such activity be confined to recognized and declared war zones and prohibited elsewhere, recognizing that brings in its train legal issues over, for example, the status and treatment of prisoners? What degree of intelligence confidence ought to be required before strikes are launched against terrorist leaders or facilities that may risk civilian collateral damage? What are ethically acceptable rules for assessing risks of collateral deaths when the fight is, in General Sir Rupert Smith's phrase, pursued among the people? Is it acceptable to make that judgement proportional to the value of the terrorist target, so allowing more civilians to be put at risk if the target is a key terrorist?

When suspected terrorists are captured outside the

---

4   See the full discussion of the US experience in P. B. Heymann and J. N. Kayyem, *Protecting Liberty in an Age of Terror* (The MIT Press: BCSIA Studies in International Security, 2005) and D. Byman, 'Do Targeted Killings Work?', *Foreign Affairs*, March/April 2006.

5   See the analysis in D. Krezmer, 'The Targeted Killing of Suspected Terrorists', *The European Journal of International Law*, Vol. 16, No. 2, 2005.

battlefield, and lack of evidence of an admissible kind does not allow for their prosecution in court, would we be justified in using secret intelligence to intern them? In our history there have been moments (as there was in 1939) when the UK Government has judged there to be sufficient national peril to justify such measures to contain those who might be potential enemies. International law today provides for proper derogation from international obligations to allow suspension of some non-absolute rights during a period of national emergency. But the logic of the approach outlined here is that it is necessary not only to show that the situation posed a sufficiently serious threat to the life of the nation but also that the proposed response would not prove counter-productive in terms of progress towards the longer-term strategy being followed. In most American eyes, 9/11 was a surprise attack and certainly a war-like emergency that justified the detention measures taken to hold suspects captured in operations in Afghanistan and elsewhere. Some years further on, the balance of argument for the strategic justification for the detention facilities at Guantanamo Bay and elsewhere[6] tips the other way, and it can be seen more clearly that continuing the detention policy (against the background of the treatment initially of detainees) now carries a high price in terms of strategic loss to set against the immediate security gains. One approach that has been explored by American jurists[7] is to have 'war zones' designated in

---

6   See, for example, the judgement in the House of Lords in December 2004 that the requirement of imminence is not expressed in Article 15 of the European Convention or Article 4 of the ICCPR but has been treated by the European Court as a necessary condition of a valid derogation. It is a view shared by the distinguished academic authors of the Siracusa Principles on the Limitation and Derogation Provisions in the International Covenant on Civil and Political Rights, who in 1985 formulated the rule: 'The principle of strict necessity shall be applied in an objective manner.. Each measure shall be directed to an actual, clear, present, or imminent danger and may not be imposed merely because of an apprehension of potential danger.' *A and Others (Appellants) v. Secretary of State for the Home Department, op. cit.*
7   Heymann and Kayyem, *op. cit.*

which rules of engagement would be set that would allow within them the capture and interrogation without legal process of suspects using coercive methods. Lethal force might also be authorized within such zones against terrorists identified by intelligence. Outside such designated war zones such methods would be prohibited. The longer-term effect of that approach is harder to judge, but it does at least represent a recognition that a problem does exist and an attempt to resolve it within a legal framework.

A related set of dilemmas arises over the close liaisons that Western governments, reasonably, are developing with the security and intelligence authorities of governments overseas that are also suffering from terrorism. What if these countries are themselves suspected of ill treatment of suspects? What is to be done with their nationals captured as part of counter-terrorist operations overseas? Can suspects be rendited back to third countries who wish to interrogate them in relation to allegations of involvement in terrorism? Additionally, can we sustain the position that British intelligence information that might identify suspects should be passed to other countries if that information might lead to action that would not be considered acceptable by the UK?

The UK military and intelligence community is subject to strict rules of engagement: the UK does not, for example, engage in assassination or torture and has very strict codes of conduct and training for those who carry out interrogations. If we consider the use of force, there are no special rules or legal authority, only the criminal law and the common-law doctrine of minimum force. We have seen this doctrine tested in the courts in Northern Ireland, holding members of the security forces accountable under the ordinary law and liable to prosecution after, say, a shooting by a soldier at a roadblock or a raid on a terrorist hide-out. No one has 007 status. So is it therefore acceptable to pass actionable intelligence we may obtain on a suspect onto a country whose rules of engagement for dealing with identified or captured terrorists is different from ours?

A persistent dilemma for the officers managing collection through covert human intelligence sources is the issue of so-called 'participating informers'.[8] It is hard to avoid the taint of having colluded in criminal acts when any well-placed agents in a terrorist organization are likely to have engaged in criminal activity or even have blood on their hands. There are moral hazards for agents and handlers alike. Nor do agents have 'Get out of jail' cards if they are, as they may be, caught breaking the law. Yet it is precisely such agents that are likely to be the key to pre-emptive intelligence needed for public safety. Great care is, I know, taken by the UK Agencies in the supervision of those concerned in such operational activities[9] and it may be that at some point legislation may be needed to give additional protection to those engaged in running such agents and clarify their legal standing – but I do not pretend that it would be at all easy to establish in legislation the limits of how far the state should go in indemnifying its officers from the consequences of their actions in such circumstances.

Accepting third-country information where there may be suspicions that it may be tainted by the methods by which it was obtained is also problematic, and certainly such evidence could never be used as part of a legal process. But the governments of other countries are most unlikely to admit (and would most probably vigorously deny) to having used torture

---

8 Some of the legal issues arising from human rights legislation are discussed in A. A. Gillespie, 'The Legal Use of Participating Informers', *Web Journal of Current Legal Issues* (Blackstone Press, webjcli.ncl.ac.uk/2000/issue5/gillespie5.html, 2005).

9 A discussion of the approach being taken by police forces is given in M. Maguire and T. John, *Intelligence, Surveillance and Informants: Integrated Approaches* (London: Home Office Police Research Group, Crime Detection and Prevention Series: Paper No. 64, 1995).

or inhuman or degrading treatment in their interrogations. Intelligence information, which may be as sparse as a telephone number or an address to check, does not come with certificates of origin. Information from liaison services overseas has, we are reliably told, led to potential attacks against British interests being thwarted. The present British policy to accept information from any source that bears on our major interests, at the same time as we take all reasonable steps to promote overseas our views over acceptable interrogation methods, therefore seems the best that can be done.

The collection and use of technical intelligence also has its share of dilemmas arising out of issues of privacy.

In modern intelligence agencies we already have very powerful capabilities for personal intrusion and for acquiring private information, and for triggering action. In seeking to sharpen the effectiveness of their intelligence establishments, governments are exploiting the latest information technology. These technical methods are proving particularly valuable in providing first clues to the existence of covert networks, but their very effectiveness is rubbing up against feelings of invasion of individual privacy, and worries over the wider uses to which such information might be put. For example, the US Administration is facing legal challenge to the steps it has taken, controversially using war powers, to harness the capability of information technology to search large volumes of personal internet communications and to monitor international financial transactions. We must expect the intelligence value of such methods to increase further, at the same time as the costs of these technologies continues to fall. Similar dilemmas arise in some European countries – for example, over the increasing use of closed-circuit surveillance cameras, already very widely deployed in the UK, or over the retention of communications data by the telecommunications companies to allow analysis by the national security authorities.

We have to accept that the realm of intelligence operations is of course a zone where the ethical rules that we might hope to govern our private conduct as individuals in society cannot fully apply. If the purpose of all intelligence is to improve decision-making by reducing ignorance, then the purpose of secret intelligence is to achieve that in respect of matters, secrets, that other people are trying hard to hide. Finding out other people's secrets is going to involve breaking everyday moral rules, the equivalent of reading others' mail, listening at and peeping through keyholes, deliberately encouraging indiscretion and inciting breaches of confidence or duty, as well as masquerading as what you are not. In addition, effectiveness against global networks requires co-operation with secret services overseas; and such liaisons will include countries whose methods we might regard as crude and ethically doubtful. Intelligence collection against terrorist and criminal networks also increasingly involves using modern information technology to sift large quantities of personal information, and that in turn raises issues of individual privacy and distaste for state prying.

In embarking on long journeys (as the struggle against jihadist terrorism will be) it is wise to have at least an outline set of directions to follow so that deviations from course can be identified. I have already mentioned the British experience that in counter-terrorism short cuts lead to long delays. It would not be a complete answer but it would help sustain confidence in the route-finding capacity of government if there were recognition that members of the British intelligence community do, as part of their everyday professional life, follow a set of ethical norms set firmly within the framework of human rights. I believe that this is the case already, implicitly, in line with both statute law and the internal instructions of the various agencies. I want to go on now to explore how one might go about trying to draw out, at least in outline, what are the ethical principles that guide British intelligence activities.

In this exercise I follow the just-war tradition[10] that provides conditions which ought to be satisfied if war is to be justly undertaken – *jus ad bellum* in the accepted shorthand; and the constraints and prohibitions that ought to be observed in the conduct of war once entered into – *jus in bello*. My thesis is that the public would value reassurance that there can also be ethical guidelines for intelligence and that they are applied by UK agencies in countering terrorism. Public support in the UK, and agreement at a European level, for necessary future developments in intelligence collection and use in reducing the risk from terrorism may come to depend upon such an understanding.

I would suggest six guidelines to govern both the purposes – the potential intelligence requirements and types of target – for which government should acquire such capabilities, *jus ad intelligentiam*, and the limitations society should place on the methods to be employed as these capabilities are unleashed, *jus in intelligentia*:

1. There must be sufficient sustainable cause.
2. There must be integrity of motive.
3. The methods to be used must be proportionate.
4. There must be right authority.
5. There must be reasonable prospect of success.
6. Recourse to secret intelligence must be a last resort.

1. There must be sufficient sustainable cause

This is a check on any tendency for the secret world to encroach into areas unjustified by the scale of potential harm to national interests that is to be prevented or advantage to be secured. If intelligence capability is to be maintained and

---

10   M. Walzer, *Just and Unjust Wars* (London: Basic Books, 1977).

developed, there has to be a sufficiently compelling purpose that can then be reflected, in British usage, in an approved set of intelligence requirements.

With such considerations in mind, in the legislation that placed the intelligence agencies on a statutory footing, the UK Parliament limited the purposes for which intelligence activities are allowed. Thus, for example, the functions of MI6 and GCHQ are legally restricted to being exercisable only:[11]

> (a) in the interests of national security, with particular reference to the defence and foreign policies of Her Majesty's Government in the United Kingdom; or (b) in the interests of the economic well-being of the United Kingdom; or (c) in support of the prevention or detection of serious crime.

In the British system approved requirements for collection within this definition are drawn up annually by the Joint Intelligence Committee and submitted to ministers along with strategic guidelines for the development of future capability. Intelligence capability does, however, take considerable time to develop, whether in terms of recruiting networks of agents or developing technical means. Much development therefore has to take place in anticipation of need, a characteristic that intelligence shares with national defence.

While describing legitimate purposes, let me acknowledge that I recognize that intelligence agencies do not just collect intelligence; they also support covert action on behalf of government. This is clearly legitimate, with examples such as using back channels to persuade a country like Libya to renounce its WMD programmes, or operating a 'sting' against terrorist groups seeking to buy surface-to-air missiles. But

---

11   Intelligence Services Act 1994 (London: HMSO).

covert action can also involve trying to follow in the dark policies that a government cannot admit to pursuing in the light. Covert policies usually get exposed eventually and can be highly controversial, generating scandals such as the US Iran-Contra affair. As with Wotan's attempts to bypass the treaties engraved on his spear-point, attempts to achieve surreptitiously by the use of controlled proxies ends that are not publicly admissible or lawful can end in Wagnerian disaster. The major issues raised by such covert operations are largely about the conduct of foreign policy by non-diplomatic means, and not about the ethics of intelligence collection itself. That, therefore, is a debate for another occasion, although I recognize that if there is international mistrust of intelligence agencies, some of that stems from the controversy over their part in past covert activity rather than collection itself. For present purposes this chapter focuses on intelligence collection and assessment for public protection and actions that can only take place because of the knowledge given by such secret intelligence. In that sense, even intelligence assessment involves actions that are susceptible to ethical scrutiny.

2. There must be integrity of motive

As writers of spy fiction like to remind us, this can be a world where all is not what it seems and case-officers can become lost in a wilderness of mirrors, in the words of James Jesus Angleton's famous borrowing.[12] Are the motives of all concerned in a proposed operation what they appear? And is there integrity in the recruitment of human sources, who

---

12 The phrase comes from T. S. Eliot's 'Gerontion' in *Poems* (1920) and was used by Angleton to describe the world of double and triple agents of the Cold War. The poem also expresses the counter-intelligence officer's dilemma: 'What will the spider do, suspend its operations, will the weevil delay?'

must be convinced that their identity and interests will be protected?

Following this guideline should involve public assurance that there is proper concern with the integrity of the whole system throughout the intelligence process, from collection through to the analysis, assessment and presentation of the resulting intelligence. Governments are too often accused these days of having hidden agendas, not least in their presentation of the terrorist threat to the public. Any guidelines for the intelligence community must, for example, make clear that there is no possibility of political authority being misused. If we take what is probably the most sensitive area for the UK, the Security Service's intelligence gathering at home, unlike most areas of government[13] the minister is not statutorily personally responsible and therefore cannot give operational directions. The authority to direct domestic operations is vested directly in the Director General, and not ministers, precisely in order to avoid any perception of the misuse of the power of their office by ministers for political or personal purposes. As part of 'right authority' (Guideline 4 below), the Secretary of State is, however, accountable to Parliament (that is, may be held to render an account rather than be held personally responsible) for the operations of the Service. Since the Director General is appointed by the Secretary of State, that provides a counter-balancing means of ultimate democratic control.

There is certainly one ethical norm that should apply to all intelligence work, and that is integrity in presenting the results to customers for intelligence. Whatever the arts of deception (the 'trade-craft' in the jargon), the reader must have complete

---

13 Under the 'Carltona' principle, British civil servants act using the authority of their minister, who therefore retains responsibility for their actions in his/her name.

confidence in the integrity of the system that delivered the intelligence. The greatest sin for an intelligence officer, as it is for the scientist, is to betray the integrity of professional method. The results must not be massaged to fit prejudices or prevailing orthodoxies, or to avoid offending the prevailing political climate. Negative results must be reported as well as positive scoops, and every result must have associated with it the error estimate and the degree of reliability. Such issues were central to the independent review (the Butler Inquiry) set up by the British Government in 2004 into intelligence on weapons of mass destruction. One key finding by Lord Butler's committee was indeed that there had been weaknesses in the effective application and resourcing of validation procedures to scrutinize human intelligence sources,[14] and that helped explain the problems of unreliable or questionable intelligence on Iraqi WMD. All of this is setting a very high standard, but assurance of integrity of the workings of our intelligence community has to remain at the heart of the profession of intelligence.

I would highlight one particular application of this guideline that is essential to building public trust in the use of intelligence for public protection. When and how should secret intelligence about terrorist activity be revealed to the public? Here, to have public trust in integrity of motive is essential. We should expect to be given public warnings related to threats that are being uncovered by intelligence when to do so would enable the public to take action that would reduce the risk to themselves and their interests (thus, for example, through following warnings of threats overseas given on the Foreign and Commonwealth Office website). We already have assurances from ministers to that effect. But we should remember that the

---

14   R. Butler, *Review of Intelligence on Weapons of Mass Destruction* (London: House of Commons HC 898, 2004).

best chance of reducing the risk to the public is to follow the leads and uncover the whole conspiracy. Counter-terrorist operations involve significant nerve to be kept on the part of the police and intelligence staff alike as they manage the risks involved, and they have to be trusted to have as their sole motive the protection of the public, now and in the future, and not considerations of media presentation or political climate.

We have to accept, however, that public reassurance about the detail of intelligence sources and methods against terrorism is hard to provide given understandable concerns to protect intelligence sources and methods. But if we cannot responsibly give the public a full explanation of the inwardness of some of the proposals for counter-terrorist measures and operations, then the public has to be invited to consider only the principles and take quite a lot of the detail on trust. Such trust in the ethics of intelligence collection, and trust in the integrity of all those involved in the intelligence community is, however, it has to be said, still problematic after the controversy over the use of intelligence in the run-up to the war in Iraq, and given controversy over the conduct of some current counter-terrorist operations.

3. The methods to be used must be proportionate

This guideline is perhaps the most fundamental for those managing and approving intelligence operations. Is the likely impact of the proposed intelligence-gathering operation taking account of the methods to be used in proportion to the seriousness of the business in hand in terms of the harm that it seeks to prevent – for example, by using only the minimum intrusion necessary into the private affairs of others?

By the impact of a human intelligence operation I include the nature of the agent recruitment and inducements, the physical risks involved, and the moral hazard to agent and handler alike, particularly where participating informants are being run. These are matters that are largely governed in the UK by internal regulation within the intelligence community rather than by statute. For technical intelligence operations, in assessing proportionality under this guideline, the impact must also be judged in terms of the extent of intrusion into personal affairs or family privacy. In this area, there is full legislative coverage in the UK. The Regulation of Investigative Powers Act 2000 (RIPA), for example, already embodies the principle of proportionality through differing levels of request and approval. In other words, the test for those approving bugging and eavesdropping operations is of minimum necessary intrusion[15] comparable to the common law doctrine of 'minimum necessary force'.

Does this principle of proportionality mean that, provided the right hoops were gone through, any method, however extreme, would be justified for gathering intelligence on the most serious of threats? What solution are we to give consistent with these proposed guidelines – for example, to the often-quoted (so far hypothetical) torture conundrum of what is to be done with the captured terrorist believed to know the location of the nuclear device about to explode? Should the guidelines be interpreted to mean *in extremis* allowing torture, or allowing coercive means that might amount to 'cruel, inhuman or degrading treatment'[16] (methods currently prohibited to UK agencies)? Can it be argued that extreme circumstances (hundreds of thousands of lives at stake) would justify such means to extract the information from the suspect?

---

15   R. V. Jones, *Reflections on Secret Intelligence* (London: Mandarin, 1989).
16   Such as the six techniques of hooding, sleep deprivation, wall standing, restrictions on food and water, and white noise, which were banned by the UK following the adverse finding of the European Human Rights Court: Ireland v. United Kingdom, 25 Eur. Ct. HR (ser.A) (1978).

I think not. There is one absolute right that has international recognition, and that is the prohibition on torture.[17]
Such a firm rule cannot have a *force majeure* let-out clause to
be invoked when the stakes are high without vitiating the role
of ethical guidelines. It is not necessary, and indeed it is
harmful overall, to try to produce as part of a code of ethics a
'strict necessity' let-out allowing the code itself to be set aside
when the stakes are high enough, either in the view of the
officers directly concerned or of their superiors, including ministers. We cannot have ethical guidelines that cease to apply
when it could be argued they are most needed.

There is also another argument that means that the ethical
guidelines exercise need not be derailed by having to cover the
hardest cases such as 'ticking bomb' scenarios. We have to
recognize that individuals still retain the freedom to guide their
own actions as free moral agents. If they choose to operate
outside their guidelines – just as if a soldier in Northern
Ireland had individually chosen to open fire *in extremis*
outside the 'Yellow Card' that contains the essence of their
rules of engagement – they know they will be answerable at
law. They know, too, that they would have to justify their
actions afterwards before the court of public opinion and their
own conscience if they survive. If they had decided to play
outside the rules, then they would have to face the possible
legal consequences. Equally, and importantly in the case in
question of the terrorists with a nuclear weapon, the individuals concerned would also have to justify any inaction. They
would not be entitled and should not expect to be allowed to
use the secrecy of their profession to evade accountability. Nor
could they mount a 'Nuremburg defence' of following orders
since there is no duty to follow an unlawful order, and no

---

17   Convention against Torture and Other Cruel, Inhuman or Degrading
Treatment or Punishment, 10 December 1984, 1465 UNTS 85.

government could authorize itself to give such an unlawful order. In the highly unlikely event of having to face such a scenario in which hundreds of thousands of lives were at stake from the 'ticking bomb' and there was such a chance of preventing it through interrogation, I would expect senior ministers to tell the security authorities that they would defend in Parliament and in court any action that the officers on the spot felt personally to be acceptable to them and necessary to secure the vital information and prevent disaster. That would not, I emphasize, make any unlawful order lawful. However, armed with such a 'letter of comfort', the individuals concerned in such an extraordinary situation might well trust the prosecuting authorities, and if it came to it the courts, to recognize in mitigation the public interest in their actions *in extremis*. But what they could not have under the sort of ethical guidelines I suggest is pre-emptive legal absolution. Hard cases make bad law, and we should not build our ethical guidelines on the extreme case.

4. There must be right authority

The issue here is whether it can be demonstrated that for sensitive intelligence-gathering activities there is a proper authorizing process at a sufficiently senior level, and with accountability within a chain of command. Additionally, in terms of public confidence that this is indeed the case, there is the need for proper oversight from outside the intelligence community and a robust mechanism whereby any individual issues of conscience or concern within the community can be raised without fear, yet in ways that will protect the essential secrecy of the business.

The most sensitive area is probably that of domestic surveillance. For this category of intrusive operations, the Britsh public can, I hope, take reassurance that, as I indicated above, the relevant Act – RIPA 2000 – carefully calibrates both those who may request intrusive operations and the level of seniority of those approving them. The position of the Secretary of State at the apex of approval for the warranting of the most intrusive operations provides him and the key officials in his department with insight into the day-to-day activities of the agencies. At the same time, as I have explained, the statute has safeguards against political interference in operations. A very British constitutional settlement.

The extent of judicial oversight of the activities of the UK intelligence community is, I suspect, not sufficiently recognized. A senior judge is appointed as Intelligence Services Commissioner under RIPA 2000 to keep under review the issue of warrants by the Secretary of State authorizing eavesdropping and interference with property and the use by the Security Service of covert human intelligence sources in accordance with the requirements of the law.[18] In addition, RIPA 2000 provides for another senior judge to act as Interception of Communications Commissioner[19] with responsibility to keep under review the issue of interception warrants by the Secretary of State.

More generally, for the oversight of the expenditure, administration and policy of the secret intelligence agencies, Parliament has legislated[20] for the cross-party Intelligence and Security Committee (ISC), drawn from both Houses of Parliament. The ISC works within 'the ring of secrecy' with, in the course of an investigation, access to senior agency staff and to

---

18　The Commissioner's annual report is presented to Parliament – see, for example, http://www.official-documents.co.uk/document/hc0506/hc05/0548/0548.pdf.

19　Report of the Interception of Communications Commissioner 2004, http://www.archive2.official-documents.co.uk/document/deps/hc/hc883/883.pdf.

20　In the Intelligence Services Act, 1994.

classified information. The ISC is therefore in practice in a position to provide Parliament with informed reassurance on the ethical standards being applied, and to draw attention to issues it uncovers.

5. There must be reasonable prospect of success

Intelligence operations carry risks, and before approval is given there has to be a judgement that the impact if the operation were to be exposed is acceptable. Even if the purpose is valid (Guideline 1) and the methods to be used are proportionate to the issue (Guideline 3), there needs to be a hard-headed risk assessment: of risk to the operatives, to future operations of that nature, to institutional reputations. And the authorizing authority has to weigh the risks of unintended consequences, or of political or diplomatic damage if exposed, and judge them acceptable – including applying the golden rule, 'Do unto others as you would be done by'.

It has for many years (since the infamous Commander Crabb affair)[21] been the practice in the UK that the Foreign Office must be consulted about operations by any of the agencies where there are risks of diplomatic damage so that officials, or in major cases the Foreign Secretary himself, can judge whether to authorize the operation. This practice is widely known and we have to accept that intelligence activity, if discovered, will be assumed to have been carried out in the name of Her Majesty's Government. We have thereby reduced the force of any complaint we might make over other nations caught conducting comparable intelligence operations against us. Whatever the public diplomacy, the practice of espionage is

---

21   The botched and fatal frogman operation of 19 April 1956 to inspect the hull of the Soviet cruiser *Ordzhonikidze* in Portsmouth harbour that resulted in the resignation of the Chief of SIS.

widespread, including the use of diplomatic immunity, and is not going to change. The 'golden rule' in such circumstances is therefore worth following as a guide.

6. Recourse to secret intelligence must be a last resort

I include this guideline as a reminder that, for any individual line of intelligence gathering, it has to be asked whether there is no reasonable alternative way of acquiring the information from less sensitive or non-secret sources, and thus avoid all the possible moral hazards and trade-offs that collecting secret intelligence may involve. In another sense, of course, collecting open information and, where justified, secret intelligence should always be the first, and resort to armed force the last, resort of government. Secret intelligence is also expensive – and makes demands on a very scarce human resource – and on those grounds alone, even without invoking ethical considerations, should not be sought if there are open ways of obtaining the information needed.

Ethical guidelines of the kind I have outlined in this chapter are both a summary of the rules being followed and a reminder in hard cases of the tests to be applied, and that we should be encouraging other nations to follow. In the end, however, guidelines cannot be more than that. We have to recognize the difficulty of the decisions and balancing acts we expect from our Government servants, and trust to the individual judgements and conscience of those concerned. The British approach to legislation and to the management of these ethical issues has helped British Agencies build up a powerful ethos of being highly effective yet (in part because) law abiding. Means are held to matter here, as well as ends. Strict control over operational activity up their chains of command, and political authorization of sensitive activities that might have diplomatic repercussions with overseas governments, are coupled with appropriate mechanisms in place to prevent abuse of power and abuse of the secrecy of the intelligence world.

This is not, however, an area where any complacency would be justified. There are dilemmas facing the intelligence community in responding to pressure for better pre-emptive intelligence for public security against terrorism. Opinion across the Islamic world and beyond has already been stirred by the handling of some of these issues, and additional seeds of future radicalization may be being sown, including here at home. For a struggle against terrorism that has to take place among the people, whose support is needed to sustain the campaign, that would be a high price. That is what I have referred to as the sustainability part of the exercise. It is a hard test in realpolitik as well as in ethics.

8

Ethics and Intelligence

Kevin Tebbit

I have been placed in a very difficult position here because I don't fundamentally disagree with either Michael Quinlan or David Omand about the importance of an ethical basis for intelligence operations. My credentials for being here* are that for four months of this year I found myself reviewing a foreign government's external intelligence agencies, and wrote a 50- or 60-page report about them which can't be made public, but which provided for me quite a number of insights into these issues. I should say from the start that it wasn't the United States Government, so what I have to say will not refer to the United States.

I confess to feeling slightly uneasy about the nature of this debate, and the reason I'm uneasy about it is for the very point that secret intelligence is supposed to be secret. That is to say, the operations and methods and techniques employed by intelligence services in going about their tasks are to some degree impaired by open public debate about them. That is inevitable. Therefore we have a really difficult balance to strike, it seems to me, which is another balance, in addition to the ones that have been talked about, as to how far to go in seeking to

---

*The Mile End Institute session on 'Ethics and Intelligence', Queen Mary, University of London, 26 June 2006.

convince the public that the operations of their intelligence agencies are indeed in line with what people would expect them to be, not just in law, but also in terms of ethics.

So it is important to be clear about the nature of the concerns. Are these the concerns of lots of academics who are interested in the subject and want to know more about it for some sort of internal thrill? Are these the concerns of fringe minorities who enjoy debating these issues? Or are these actually essential to the credibility, legitimacy and the conduct of intelligence operations?

Having reviewed a foreign intelligence agency quite recently, I've been struck by a number of points. My basic conclusion was not that they lacked an ethical or a legal basis for activities: quite the reverse. What I found was just how concerned the members of those agencies were to be clear about what their own framework was and what their own limitations were, the ones that society wanted to place on them. I didn't find cowboys, I didn't find people wanting to ride roughshod over ethical issues or human rights, I actually found very moral people. When you think about it, intelligence professionals are likely to be that way because they have to face those issues in a rather more stark way than most of us do thinking about them academically. Now this doesn't amount to a philosophy of 'I'm an intelligence agent, trust me', but it is important to understand the context in which the intelligence agencies go about their work in reality. They need to be satisfied, more than anybody else, that they're operating within an accepted body of guidelines; and the idea that we need to impose such a framework on them is, I think, a mistake.

The other thing I found was that, far from, as it were, cutting loose and not observing ethical norms, there was a different problem, and the problem was, basically, that most intelligence agencies these days are not equipped to meet and face the challenges that twenty-first-century threats pose in their work of safeguarding national and international security interests. By and large, intelligence agencies today are still far too compartmentalized, both within their countries and in terms of international co-operation. They are not able to exchange information as freely as they should between each other about suspects, about trends, about developments. They are not able to hold enough information which the twenty-first-century world generates all the time, in every other walk of life, to enable them to use databanks as effectively as they should to carry out their work. In many ways the modern terrorist environment that David Omand was describing is very much like the Cold War, in one specific sense: of trying to work out what the opponents are up to. In the Cold War we couldn't decipher what they actually said because they used very robustly coded systems and it was impossible to work it out. What we could do was to build up patterns and under-stand patterns of behaviour so that if these patterns diverged from the norm, we knew something was up and could take precautionary measures accordingly.

The current world of counter-terrorism requires the use of similar techniques but the process of collecting and sharing the information which is required in order to do that is regarded by many people as infringing their privacy. In my view, we need to change the terms of the debate to enable necessary intelligence-gathering operations to go forward. There are, as I say, big inhibitions for most intelligence agencies throughout the world about doing that sort of thing. Their legal base has often not kept pace with the pace of technology and modern systems out there in communications. That is a major example of what I mean.

So rather than see problems of ethics – and I don't under-estimate the importance of managing these for the sake of the intelligence agencies themselves as well as for the external world – I see more practical problems about the conduct of legitimate intelligence to meet the threats we have, and I would hope very much that the debate here and in other places does not become so intrusive as to impair further the ability of intelligence agencies to go about their business.

I think you can classify these issues into three areas. First, what are the targets, what are the objectives of the intelligence agency? What is it that is sufficiently important to justify on occasion people breaking what is otherwise regarded as the law? I think that is relatively straightforward: governments decide this; Richard Mottram, as the senior responsible official, is involved in the process on not a daily but a regular basis; there are proper prioritized lists that exist in all countries of what government as a whole has decided it wants secret intelligence to provide on the basis that it cannot either get it, or needs to have it amplified, from open sources. There is a very important principle, which I think David enunciated, that these things need not to be available by other means to justify using secret intelligence methods.

The more difficult area is how you go about doing it, which raises the most delicate aspects, as we have discussed. The third area, the intelligence product itself, is, I think, a slightly easier issue to handle in terms of the public interest.

Clearly, much of the public debate has been stimulated by Iraq and the problems of the intelligence used there, and I do think there are areas where intelligence agencies can go further in helping to ease concerns about, as it were, the quality of the evaluation. That's not just about intelligence agencies, it's about the overall intelligence community and about the assessments that are done.

In the country that I was reviewing – and I can now say it was Denmark because eventually some of my conclusions were published by the Danish Government – their intelligence agencies, the equivalent effectively to the JIC, publish an unclassified assessment of their judgement of the threats facing

Denmark. It's done at the same time each year to avoid it appearing to be affected or influenced by the political process and it is offered to the Danish Parliament, the Danish Government, the Danish people at the same time, and there is a debate in the Danish Parliament about it. I think it is a very healthy way of trying to demystify some of these things. It doesn't go into methods of collection and techniques, but it does, I think, help to inform debate about why it is important for intelligence agencies to go about their business and, broadly speaking, what it is they find.

Similarly, before the Danish Government commits to sending forces to Afghanistan and Iraq – in other words, deliberately putting their citizens directly in harm's way – again the intelligence agencies, their equivalent of the JIC, provide an unclassified assessment of the threats and the risks and the benefits to be gained, which are debated in the Danish Parliament and provide the basis to the debate for both Government and opposition. And I think that, in that way, the Danish authorities are helping to build and rebuild confidence among a public which has traditionally been rather sceptical about the operations of secret intelligence, given their national emphasis on liberty and individual rights.

So, I think David is on the right track. The six principles he enunciated are right and proper. But I would just caution that one does have to be extremely careful not to throw out the baby with the bathwater. There are rules to be heeded on how countries go about collecting intelligence, but in some respects these need to be relaxed in the interests of our own security. How to achieve that? I venture to suggest that in exchange for enabling intelligence agencies to exploit the benefits of technology that the terrorists and other criminals themselves use, there could be stronger oversight arrangements to protect the public interest – oversight provided by senior judges, for example, examining everything that goes on and giving confidence that this has been properly conducted. You don't have to rely on officials even outside the intelligence agency to tell you that it's proper and OK: you can rely on judicial and confidential Parliamentary arrangements too, and I think we will need to call on those sorts of oversight because not everything can be exposed to the general public gaze.

In any event, I do not believe that the right way forward is to provide many more details in public about the operations and the methods that are necessarily used by the intelligence agencies, or to assume that the people we charge with responsibility for this duty are operating in an environment that is less principled or ethical than the one lived in by society as a whole.

Epilogue

Peter Hennessy

Will the thinking and the analyses contained within these pages swiftly date? Impossible to know. Certainly the UK as a whole is still adjusting to what Matthew d'Ancona, the Editor of *The Spectator*, in October 2006 called the 'psychological shrapnel' of a 'cold sweat war' intended 'not only to cause bloodshed but also . . . to disfigure normality, to desecrate the routine' and to deploy 'weapons [which] range from outright terror to the most irrational suspicion . . . a war in which the enemy seeks, more than in any other, to get inside our heads as much as to mutilate our bodies'.[1]

The biggest surprise of all, however, would be if the threat from international terrorism proved short-lived. The shared assessment of the contributors to this book is that it will not and that, as a country, the UK faces durable, mutating dangers that will stretch the human and physical resources of the British intelligence community, and the protective state of which it is a crucial part, to the full.

The Mile End Group and the Mile End Institute are immensely grateful to the serving and retired practitioners who have pooled their thinking in this book. And the intention of the Mile Enders is, between them, to continue observing and analysing the new protective state in action.

---

1 Matthew d'Ancona, 'Confessions of a Hawkish Hack: The Media and the War on Terror', The Philip Geddes Memorial Lecture delivered at St Edmund Hall, Oxford, 27 October 2006.

List of Contributors

Peter Hennessey is Attlee Professor of Contemporary British History at Queen Mary, University of London and Director of the Mile End Institute for the Study of Government, Intelligence and Society.

Sir Michael Quinlan was Permanent Under-Secretary of State at the Ministry of Defence, and Director of the Ditchley Foundation.

Sir David Omand was UK Security and Intelligence Coordinator, Permanent Secretary of the Home Office and Director GCHQ and is currently a visiting Professor at King's College London.

Sir Kevin Tebbit was Permanent Under-Secretary of state at the Ministry of Defence and served widely in policy, management and intelligence in a career spanning both the Home Civil Service and the Diplomatic Service; he is currently a Visiting Professor at Queen Mary, University of London, and advises public and private sector organisations.

Richard Mottram was appointed as Security and Intelligence Coordinator and is now Permanent Secretary, Intelligence, Security and Resilience, Cabinet Office.

Dame Eliza Mannigham-Buller was Director General of the Security Service.

Front row: David Omand, Michael Quinlan
Back row: Peter Hennessy, Richard Mottram, Kevin Tebbit

Eliza Manningham Buller (centre) with members of the
Mile End Institute

Index